you,
him,
and the
Other
Woman

Break the Love Triangle and Reclaim Your Marriage, Your Love, and Your Life

Paul Coleman, PsyD

Adamsmedia

Avon, Massachusetts

Published by
Adams Media, a division of F+W Media, Inc.
57 Littlefield Street, Avon, MA 02322. U.S.A.
www.adamsmedia.com

ISBN 10: 1-59869-895-8
ISBN 13: 978-1-59869-895-4

Printed in the United States of America.

J I H G F E D C B A

Library of Congress Cataloging-in-Publication Data
is available from the publisher.

This publication is designed to provide accurate and authoritative information with
regard to the subject matter covered. It is sold with the understanding that the publisher is not engaged in rendering legal, accounting, or other professional advice. If legal
advice or other expert assistance is required, the services of a competent professional
person should be sought.

    —From a *Declaration of Principles* jointly adopted by a Committee of the
American Bar Association and a Committee of Publishers and Associations

Many of the designations used by manufacturers and sellers to distinguish their product
are claimed as trademarks. Where those designations appear in this book and Adams
Media was aware of a trademark claim, the designations have been printed with initial
capital letters.

This book is available at quantity discounts for bulk purchases.
For information, please call 1-800-289-0963.

you,
him,
and the
Other
Woman

For Jody

contents

131

CHAPTER 9

ten conversations you're almost guaranteed to have

149

CHAPTER 10

mental and emotional fatigue: more coping strategies

introduction

Affairs aren't the worst thing that can happen in a marriage but they come darn close. As awful as they are, affairs need not be a death sentence for a couple. With the right attitude, proper tools, and key insights, couples who wish to keep their marriage alive and well after an affair can succeed.

Before the Internet took off and allowed anybody to be in touch with practically anybody, the most authoritative study revealed that about 25 percent of all married men will eventually be unfaithful as will about 15 percent of married women, according to the book *Sex in America: A Definitive Survey* by Robert T. Michael, et al. Other studies were more pessimistic, and the percentages are higher for nonmarried couples living together. But as the twenty-first century is well under way, statistics must now take into consideration cyber-affairs— something unheard-of fifteen years ago. Many people who would never have a traditional affair that involved sneaking out to meet up with a paramour have discovered that online sex is a compelling alternative. *And many who engage in it convince themselves they really aren't cheating!* So the new numbers are fuzzy and varying, but most researchers agree that marriages are more at risk for infidelity than ever before.

But the good news is this: if your husband has had—or is having—an affair, and if both of you deep down want your marriage to survive and heal, you can make that happen. You may be thinking, "I can never get over this . . . I'll never trust him again . . . Once a cheater always a cheater . . . Our marriage is forever scarred even if we stay together." But couples who persevere to repair the marriage often discover that those beliefs are founded upon fear, hurt, and anger. Reality can be quite different.

But you also might be wondering, "What if I'm not sure I want him back? Or what if he's unsure how he feels about working things out?" That is the most common scenario I see in my work as a relationship therapist. Yes, occasionally a couple comes in and the husband is completely distraught over his affair. He'll do anything—anything—to win back her trust and devotion. But more often what I hear is ambivalence. One or both partners are uncertain what they want to have happen. He may still have feelings for his mistress. The wife may be unsure she can cope with the ups and downs of trying to work things out, or she is convinced that if he had an affair he must not love her and that the whole marriage has been a lie. So they stagger along, taking two steps forward and one or more steps backward, weighing themselves down with anger, guilt, despair, fear, and confusion as to what to do next.

In my clinical experience, more marriages fail (after an infidelity) from a couple's mismanagement of their attempt to repair and heal the relationship than from the infidelity itself. And that makes sense. The typical couple can barely handle a long day or two in the car with young kids driving to a far-off vacation spot. Why should they instinctively know how to navigate through such a complicated and emotionally painful process as repairing a marriage after infidelity? There are always pitfalls and sand traps awaiting even the most determined couples.

The trick is knowing what they are, where to find them, and how to overcome them. That's what this book is about. In this book you will learn how to:

- Process the terrible news.
- Manage overwhelming emotions.
- Talk with your "wandering" spouse in the most effective ways possible.
- Understand the nature of "love triangles"—how they develop and how they disintegrate.
- Handle possible encounters with the other woman.
- Take constructive—not destructive—action.
- Decide whether or not the marriage can be saved.
- Move forward confidently, no matter what happens.

Plenty of women have affairs. And this book can be useful for anyone whose partner has cheated—whether you are a man or woman, gay or straight. But on average more men than women cheat, so this book approaches the issue as if the woman were the hurt partner. Many unfaithful partners may claim, "Hey, I was hurt too!" No debate from me. Affairs happen for complicated reasons, and many times both spouses have had their share of hurts.

If you read this book with an open mind and an open heart, you may be surprised to find that you can overcome the pain of betrayal and move on confidently with your life.

getting a grip: handling the aftershock

When Mike called his wife Jen to say he'd be working late again, he was unaware that she answered her cell phone in the parking lot near his office. "I'll see you when you get home," Jen said. Minutes later Mike exited the building with a female coworker and Jen followed them. It didn't take long for her suspicions to be confirmed. Jen's mind raced. How long had this been going on? When Mike insisted he bring his laptop on their vacation last month, was that so he could e-mail *her?* More important, could the marriage be saved? Did she even *want* to save it? Should she confront them now? Should she tell *her* off? Jen's head spun and her heart ached. *Too many questions, not enough answers . . .*

When a relationship is devastated by betrayal, it's as if the world turns topsy-turvy—nothing makes sense anymore. What once was genuine now is unreal; what was good now seems bad. Truths were really lies, devotion was manipulation, and promises were empty words. *Or were they?*

"That's the problem when you've been lied to and betrayed," a woman said to me in therapy. "I can't be absolutely sure of anything anymore!"

You may be feeling desperate for any advice that will help you get past the pain you are in right now. Please hold fast to the belief that this problem is temporary and at some point in the future you really will have recovered.

At that time your marriage may be thriving, it may still need work, or it may be over. But emotionally you will be in a better place even if your life is not where you'd hoped it would be. People adapt. You won't always be feeling the way you are right at this moment.

Sudden Impact

In the days following the revelation of an affair your emotions will run the gamut. In fact, many betrayed spouses suffer symptoms associated with post-traumatic stress disorder. They include:

- Shock and numbness
- Appetite and sleep disturbances
- Obsessive preoccupation with the event along with attempts to rid it from your mind
- Sudden "flashbacks" that may involve witnessing the couple together, recalling the moment your first learned of the affair, or even images you created in your mind of your spouse and his lover together in some sort of romantic or sexual interlude
- Overreaction to events that should not create such a response (for example, crying or screaming when you drop something)
- Underreaction to daily events—going through the motions as if in a daze
- Emotionally reacting to "triggers" that remind you of the affair (driving by the hotel they used, seeing his cell phone bill with her number on it, and so forth)
- An overriding sense of loss and grief

In addition, you end up fighting yourself, trying to overcome the contradictions that swarm inside you. For example, you can be emotionally numb and also hypersensitive. You can be easily distracted and yet overvigilant, exhausted but unable to sleep. You will have moments of feeling love for him, followed by hating him. All of those responses make you wonder if you are going crazy. What's happening is that your mind is trying to make sense of what occurred and it is unable to sort through all of the apparent contradictions of your situation that were just listed. This is normal although very exhausting. There is a powerful method to help your mind get past all the confusion (found in Chapter 4). For now, simply know that you are *not* crazy.

As the days and weeks wear on, your many emotions will still fluctuate. But on some days one emotion may predominate. If your primary attitude is:

- *"My heart is broken"*: you are experiencing grief and perhaps the loss of a sense of being lovable.
- *"I'm scared"*: you are feeling helpless and a loss of control over what is happening.
- *"I'm disgusted"*: you are feeling anger and contempt and don't feel so helpless, but you may be overlooking your grief.
- *"I don't know what to do"*: you are feeling of loss of power and self-esteem. You have lost some faith in yourself to be able to cope.
- *"I feel humiliated"*: you have lost a sense of self-worth, or long-standing personal insecurities have been brought to the surface.
- *"It's all my fault"*: you have lost sight of why affairs happen and you feel guilty and afraid.
- *"I can't stand it!"*: you are operating under the false assumption that you will never recover, and you may have a history of not taking care of your own needs as well as you should.

If I had to sum up in one word what you experience emotionally after your spouse has an affair it is this: grief. You may not have lost the marriage, but the marriage has lost its innocence and you've lost your faith in him and your future. That faith will need to be restored if the marriage is to survive or if you are to be able to trust again. However, all grief can be lessened and much grief can pass away. This book is designed to help you find your way through that maze and come out whole on the other side.

Crushed Assumptions

When you feel reasonably happy and content with your life, you make certain assumptions about yourself, your marriage, and life in general. You feel fairly lovable and worthwhile, your spouse is your trusted friend and lover, and your future seems reasonably secure. And then "it" happens. And for a while anyway nothing is the same as it was.

Assumptions about Yourself

Before the affair you had an identity. That included not just your role (spouse, mother, profession) but how you viewed yourself. You saw yourself as worth loving, worth having. It takes a strong self-esteem to still view yourself as worthwhile after a spouse has an affair. Many people feel inadequate and "less than." They compare themselves to the other woman and obsess over how they fell short. If they view the other woman as younger or more attractive, they feel defective and disposable. If they view the other woman as possessing unappealing qualities compared to their own, that doesn't make them feel any better. One woman said, "If he chose her over me—and I know I have more to offer—there is no possible way to fix that. Maybe there's something horrible about me that I'm not even aware of." If the hurt spouse doesn't know the other woman, she may go to great lengths to find out who that woman is and what she looks like. It can turn into an obsession as she tries to determine "who I'm up against."

The decision to stay in the marriage and try to work things out can also adversely affect some women's sense of themselves. "I always told myself that if my husband had an affair I'd leave him. But now that I'm in that situation, I'm not so sure." These women might regard themselves in a positive light—as devoted spouses willing to at least try to forgive. But they also may regard themselves as foolish or unwilling to stand up for their long-held beliefs. If so, the question "Who am I, really?" looms large. Women who viewed themselves as even-tempered, strong, and fair-minded now watch themselves as in a movie, behaving in ways they never thought possible and out of control of their emotions.

Self-blame is also common. On the surface a betrayed wife might thoroughly blame her husband for his affair, but inwardly she worries that she may be at fault. Somehow she neglected her husband in some way or made a horrible mistake in judgment by marrying him in the first place. (Part of that thinking comes from the fact that women more than men tend to take more responsibility for how others feel and act. When a marriage is faltering, it is more often the wife who tries harder to keep things afloat.) The self-blaming is intensified when the husband justifies his affair by pointing out his wife's personal or sexual inadequacies. The wife might argue back and accuse him of making excuses but still be unable to let go of the idea that had she acted differently in the marriage his affair might have been avoided. This can lead to intense guilt and feelings of inadequacy—especially if children are involved and the marriage may not survive.

Assumptions about Your Husband

He may not have been perfect but you never thought he would cheat on you. Unless you already saw him as selfish, abusive, or a philanderer, you probably held him in some sort of positive regard. Now that he's betrayed you, you wonder what else about him you have no clue about. When he told you he loved you, was he ever being honest? Maybe you regard him as a "good" father. Now you see that a divorce is a possibility. How will that affect the children? You wonder, *Didn't he care about that? Did he even think about that?*

Evelyn learned of her husband's cheating when she noticed lesions on her genitals. Her gynecologist diagnosed an STD. "I felt totally humiliated," she said. "When my doctor told me I should be tested for other sexually transmitted diseases I wanted to crawl under a rock." Later, Evelyn realized that her husband put her health at risk. "What kind of man would do that? I thought he at least cared enough about me to protect me."

Evelyn felt disgusted by her husband's affair. But when she sorted through old photographs of the two of them happy together, she felt more confused than ever. "If he was a good man before, can he still be a good man? Did he just make a terrible mistake or does this tell me something fundamental about his character? I just don't know."

As a partial protection against pain, people often develop black-and-white thinking after a crisis. The husband's actions are forgivable—or they aren't. He's still a good person—or he's completely

7

untrustworthy. Such thinking keeps people out of the gray areas of life where there is much more confusion and uncertainty. But since life and human actions are rarely so cut-and-dried, black-and-white thinking is not an effective way to look at things over the long term.

Assumptions about Life and Your Future

Typically, the effort to learn "why" the affair happened is a frustrating and complicated process for couples. (That will be discussed at length in the next chapter.) The upshot for you when you've been betrayed is that you may not know for sure why your husband strayed. His answers seem too vague ("It just happened"), incomplete ("I didn't think it through"), or just not good enough ("I realized I wasn't happy"). Because you have no clear understanding of why the affair took place, you have a hard time seeing a future that is safe and predictable. And if divorce is likely, then your future can seem scary since lifestyle changes will almost certainly occur.

You may also find yourself at odds with your past assumptions about life. You may have thought that if you tried to live a decent life, you could avoid many painful experiences. You may have regarded some other wives as less devoted to their husbands than you were, and yet your husband cheated on you while their husbands did not cheat on them. And if you seek counsel and are told to find a way to forgive, you may come away feeling not at all understood. (Even when you wish to find forgiveness, it's always helpful for someone who is listening to you to let you know that your feelings of rage and betrayal make sense. Hasty advice to "Make your marriage work" may be well-intended but often misses the mark. Similarly, advice from friends to "Get rid of him!" may also fail to help you feel understood.)

This eruption of mixed emotions and confusion about how to think eventually lessens in intensity. But it is most apparent during the initial phase of coping with infidelity.

The Phases of Recovery

Whether you and your spouse remain together or not, you can expect to go through three phases as you cope with the impact of the affair:

1. The roller coaster phase
2. The subdued phase
3. The rebuilding phase

These phases can vary in duration and intensity and they tend to overlap. However, one phase usually predominates at any given time. Don't judge how you are doing compared with others you know who've had to cope with an affair. Some people are extremely emotional, others almost paralyzed, and others seem to manage their feelings with fewer emotional peaks and valleys. There are too many factors at work as to why you are reacting the way you are. You possess a different personality and a different background than others. Your coping skills can be different.

The Roller Coaster Phase

This phase typically lasts for one to six months although the intensity and frequency of the emotional ups and downs tends (thankfully) to settle down over time. The initial four to eight weeks can be the most intense. Then emotions often run wild. The marriage is in crisis—much like an area devastated by a tornado is in crisis—and emotions swirl for those involved. It is an exhausting phase because just when you think the situation is calmer and more manageable the tornado whips up again. Here couples may argue intensely, the betrayed spouse asks question after question—never completely satisfied that she has the entire story. They don't know how to act around each other. Should he show affection? Give her space? Leave? What if he doesn't show her attention and she wants it? Marge and Bob were married for ten years when Bob had a four-month affair. The affair ended and Bob wanted his marriage to work. In bed at night he'd reach over to Marge to offer comfort. She'd jerk her body away, her way of saying "Don't you dare touch me!" Bob held back for a few nights and then tried again. Marge had none of it. Eventually he stopped altogether; he feared alienating her even further. In our session, Marge expressed how annoyed she was that Bob stopped trying to hold her at night.

"But you kept pushing me away!" Bob protested.

Marge answered, "Just because I push you away twelve times in a row doesn't mean I don't want you to try a thirteenth time."

Phil came to my office shortly after his affair was exposed. His wife Terry was disgusted with him. Her fury seemed to know no bounds. Phil had dark circles under his eyes from sleepless nights. His wife would awaken him, barraging him with more questions, demanding answers. When he responded "I don't know" or "I don't remember" his wife became even more irate. He sat across from me, unable anymore to fight back the tears. "I can't convince her . . . I don't know what to do . . . I don't want to lose her."

The roller coaster phase is tough on both partners. The hurt spouse may have little sympathy for her wandering husband but that doesn't change the fact that this phase can be torturous for him, too. As the phase progresses it becomes clearer that the spouse who is more invested in preserving the marriage actually *has less power*. The spouse who is most unsure or who is leaning more toward exiting the marriage has more control over what happens: progress proceeds at the pace of the slowest individual.

In a marriage where both partners want the marriage to work, the power balance still shifts—sometimes hourly. One might get fed up and claim the marriage is over, sending the other into an emotional tailspin. Then the other finally agrees and says, "If that's what you want, that's what we'll do," making the "fed-up" spouse suddenly anxious and uncertain, protesting, "Wait, let's not make any rash decisions." Even when each spouse is dedicated to making the marriage work after an affair, there can be doubts. *Does he (or she) really mean it? Is he trying hard enough? Is she only doing this for the kids? To keep her lifestyle?* To add to the confusion, friends and relatives (and even therapists) can offer advice or make comments that only make you doubt yourself, your partner, or your decision to end the marriage or salvage it.

The Subdued Phase

When this phase is in full operation, emotions are nearly spent. The couple is exhausted. Anger, guilt, mistrust, or despair may still simmer below the surface but there is little energy or desire to contend with those emotions in an up-front manner. During the roller coaster phase, there are brief moments when calmness takes over but they usually don't last long. However, during the subdued phase a couple can go for weeks on end without much arguing. Typically the hurt spouse makes an occasional verbal jab but for the most part there is little fight left in either partner.

This phase is key. Couples can take advantage of their diminished arguing and begin the process of enjoying each other once again. But often in the early days of this phase, the battle-weary couple begins to wonder if they will ever be truly happy together. Of course they can be, but at that time they're not so sure. Their skepticism can become a self-fulfilling prophecy if they are not careful. A common attitude of an unfaithful husband during this phase is "I've paid my dues" and he has little patience for more questions, uncalled-for accusations, or cold shoulders from his wife. For her part, she may resent that she is now supposed to put the past behind her. A little understanding on each person's part can go a long way to making this phase easier to manage.

At this phase, the couple looks back at all they have been through. If all they see is wreckage, it may be hard for them to envision a bright future together. So it is important to sort through the emotional rubble and find those nuggets of gold—their positive memories, shared challenges they've successfully met, the reasons they married in the first place. This phase is the springboard for the final phase of coping.

The Rebuilding Phase

Rebuilding starts the moment you and your husband decide to commit to the marriage after his affair was revealed. However, it is hard to rebuild in earnest during the first two phases when you are stampeded by emotions and thoroughly exhausted. The primary goals of this phase are rebuilding trust and goodwill. This is accomplished by looking at areas of the relationship that are weak and improving them, or by each of you examining personal weaknesses and striving to improve them.

A mistake some couples make at this stage is to enjoy the fact that they are clearly over the major hurdles and decide to leave well enough alone. They may be afraid to keep tinkering with the marriage, fearing it might lead to more complications. Taking a "breather" now and then is fine. Abandoning efforts to make more improvements is a mistake. Of course, even with improvements there is no way to absolutely affair-proof any marriage no matter how appealing that ideal sounds. A healthy marriage is based upon trust, respect, and love. And with that comes freedom. When partners are free to make decisions and act certain ways, some people will make the wrong decision. While a strong marriage is not immune to infidelity, a weak marriage is much more at risk for adultery.

The purpose of this chapter was to help you realize that the emotional upheaval you're experiencing is normal and that healing from the pain of infidelity involves walking through three stages. Part of the first stage is examining why the affair happened in the first place, which is what the next chapter is all about.

what happened and why: sorting through the chaos in your mind

Imagine you answer your phone and the person on the other end informs you that a mutual friend died very suddenly and unexpectedly. Your first reaction would be shock and disbelief. *"This can't be!"* It won't seem real that your friend is actually gone. Then you'd immediately inquire, "What happened?" You're not simply being curious. You are in such a state of shock that your brain seeks out information—data that will answer your questions—so that you can eventually come to emotional terms with what happened. In other words, finding out "why" something so earth-shattering happened helps you accept the fact that it actually did happen. The more traumatic or life-altering the event, the more you will obsess about it, replaying it over and over in your mind. As debilitating (and torturous) as that can be, it's really your mind's way of helping you integrate the terrible news into your life. As long as it remains unreal, you will not be able to proceed with the task of grieving and moving forward.

Unfortunately, the search for answers—which is necessary to help you cope—can become an obstacle to healing and another source of pain. Since your husband cheated on you, he's also been secretive and probably even blatantly lied (the most common response after being accused of infidelity is to deny it). So how do you know for sure that his explanations for why he cheated are in fact true? Is he lying again? Is he insightful enough to even know why he did what he did? Such doubts can keep your head spinning and your heart aching.

Chances are you've already had many tense discussions with your husband about his affair, and chances are they have not gone as well as you'd like. Before you have more troublesome conversations, it can be helpful for you to understand what affairs are really all about and why they happen in the first place.

The Definition of Infidelity

Infidelity is *a violation of an agreement between partners to remain sexually and/or emotionally exclusive.* The agreement is a covenant. A covenant is a profound agreement based upon devotion and love. But as with so many definitions there are gray areas. Sure, sometimes it's a no-brainer. If he had sex with her, he cheated. But what if he developed "feelings" for her but never acted on it? What if he was flirting online with a woman from another country whom he never met and had no intention of meeting? Is viewing pornography a form of unfaithfulness? A very jealous and possessive person may accuse a spouse of infidelity for simply being friendly toward another person (usually of the opposite sex). A highly defensive person may deny that a clear act of infidelity was in fact a violation. (A husband told me once: "It wasn't cheating. I only had sex with the woman four times.") But in the majority of cases the unfaithful partner knows he did something wrong. He may not completely agree with his wife about just how bad it was, but he knows he isn't innocent.

Types of Affairs

Affairs fall into one of three categories:

1. Sexual gratification only
2. Emotional gratification only
3. Sexual and emotional gratification

Any type can be emotionally devastating to the betrayed spouse. Not surprisingly, men and women often respond differently depending upon the type of affair their spouse has. A man may have an easier time coping when his wife has an emotional affair than if her affair involved sex. A woman may have a hard time coping if her husband developed feelings for his mistress. There is statistical evidence that shows men are more likely to have an affair just for sex (although they can be quite emotionally involved, too) whereas a woman is more likely to have an affair if she is falling in love with the other man.

While coping with your husband's unfaithfulness can be gut-wrenching, the sex-only affair may be a bit less complicated than the other two to overcome (unless the husband is a philanderer or sex addict). An emotional-only affair is more complex and usually requires more work if your marriage is to heal. A long-standing affair that involves strong sexual and emotional components carries with it the greatest threat to your marriage since it is harder for your husband to end it and perhaps harder for you to contend with it.

The Sexual-Gratification Affair

This can range from a one-night stand to liaisons that last for months or years. This also includes cybersex. For some men, a one-night stand represents a weak moment. They do not regard themselves as the type of man who would cheat and may have had no intention of cheating. ("I had a few drinks . . . it just happened.") That in no way excuses their behavior. But a husband who finds his actions reprehensible and is sincerely remorseful is very likely to do all he can to repair his marriage. The prognosis is much better.

Some men are addicted to sex. That problem is beyond the scope of this book, but unless they view their addiction as a problem and get professional help, the marriage is less likely to survive.

Some men will have a lengthy sex-only affair and purposely find a woman who has no interest in forming a meaningful relationship. While he may tell you he is not in love with the other woman (and that may well be true) a lengthy sex-only affair still requires a great deal of lying and coverup to maintain. His deceit not only shatters your trust in his honesty but it acts as a barrier to intimacy (since he must avoid certain conversations that might reveal his affair or reduce his sexual availability to you) and therefore the marriage has suffered more damage.

Is Viewing Pornography a Form of Unfaithfulness?

Today, viewing pornography is more involved than simply taking a *Playboy* magazine out of a drawer and browsing through it. Graphic sexual acts are easily accessible on the Internet. The wide variety ensures that the novelty will not wear off quickly—making it more addictive. Husbands who view pornography regularly (more than an hour per week) run a risk of becoming less attracted to their spouse and bored by "routine" sex. If the wife has a strong objection to his pornography use and especially if his use involves secrecy or deceit and diverts intimacy from his wife, he has crossed a line.

Cybersex can involve the viewing of pornographic material, the online sharing of pornographic images with another, flirting or graphic sex-talk with a chat partner, or engaging in solitary sexual activity while communicating with a chat partner. Many men will downplay the seriousness of cybersex since they are not actually physically or emotionally involved with the other partner (although chat partners sometimes do agree to meet in person after establishing an online relationship). However, cybersex tends to siphon energy away from the marriage. The husband is less connected to his wife, more emotionally charged by his online pursuits, and over time he becomes less attracted to his spouse and just goes through the motions when he does have sex with her. At best it represents a withdrawal of emotional energy and devotion to the wife. Many women feel degraded when their husband engages in any form of Internet pornography or sex because they believe they have been replaced by a computer. "He'd rather chat with a stranger or get his rocks off looking at women he doesn't know than come to me. That doesn't make me feel desirable."

The Emotional Affair

If you—the married woman—were to have an affair, the chances are good that you would do so in part because you had developed feelings for the other man or perhaps felt very lonely in your marriage. An affair "just for sex" may seem tantalizing in theory but you are less likely to go that route. Consequently, if your husband is having an emotional affair you may be more worried.

In my experience, more men walk into my office today having emotional affairs than ever before. "I feel I can talk to her," one man said. "She really seems to listen and care about me. I feel important." Some men deny that these are even affairs. "We're just friends." Frequently, these affairs are with female coworkers or other women they have regular contact with. Ironically, men who have affairs with co-workers are very likely to describe their marriages as happy. So why did they stray? Three factors seem to be operating that creates the perfect storm.

1. Accessibility
2. Attractiveness or "chemistry"
3. An underlying emotional weakness or need

All three need to be in play for an emotional affair to take root. If you suspect your husband of having (at least) an emotional affair, he may very well deny that it was his intention to cheat. And that may be true. If he is like the typical man in that situation, he slowly spent more and more time with the other woman "just as a friend," began sharing more intimate details of his life with her, and found her to be a compassionate, nonjudgmental listener. Soon he looked forward to their chats or meetings, maybe even fantasized about her before falling asleep at night, yet all the while convinced himself that since "nothing happened" there was no breach of the marital contract.

Soon he realizes that not only does he find her attractive, he actually cares about her. By now he is in a bit too deep and a sexual tension has developed. He still can back away but to do so he'd have to recognize that he made a mistake and that his "we're just friends" belief was a rational-ization. So he convinces himself that it is possible to be a mature adult who maintains a close friendship with a woman he finds both physically and emotionally appealing and still remain faithful to his spouse. Now he is playing with fire but can't back away. Soon thereafter the couple finds themselves embracing, then kissing. He knows he is in over his head but finds it hard to withdraw emotionally—in part because he probably sees her every day at work and he doesn't want to hurt her.

Emotional affairs often involve a lot of cell phone conversations, text messages, and e-mails. In order to end an emotional affair, it really isn't possible to maintain the friendship. One can still be polite and civil but that's it. As you might imagine, if your husband ends his emotional affair his feelings for her might linger for some time. That may make you worried but his actions are more important right now than his feelings. As long as he stays out of her way and rebuilds his relationship with you, his feelings for her can become a nonissue over time.

The Combination Affair

An affair that's heated sexually *and* emotionally requires the most work to recover from. The longer it has gone on, the more attached the affair-couple might be. Also, many marriages suffer a drop in overall closeness and connectedness when a spouse is having an affair, whether or not the affair had yet been exposed. Since emotional and sexual exclusivity has been breached, mistrust is high and the amount of pain suffered by a betrayed spouse is also high. But the cheating husband is in a great deal of emotional pain as well. No matter whom he chooses to commit to, he must grieve the end of the other relationship. (You may have little sympathy but it probably is how he feels.)

Why Did He Cheat?

One evening a couple attended their first therapy session in an effort to work through the husband's infidelity. He'd had a three-week fling with a woman he knew he'd never see again. "She threw herself at me," he said. "I guess I liked the novelty and the attention. But it was just for sex." His wife was furious that he would risk his marriage over a woman he had no feelings for. She viewed his fling as evidence of callous disregard for their marriage and their children's future. "It's like taking our life savings and betting it on a race just because you feel like it. At least if you loved her I could understand why," she explained.

Later in the week another couple attended a therapy session. The man had been romantically involved with a woman for about six months. His wife couldn't understand why every step along the way he made a conscious choice to get more deeply involved with the other woman—to the point where he had fallen in love. "At least if it were just for sex I could understand," she said.

Each of the wives indicated she'd have had an easier time accepting the situation if her husband's affair was of a different type. But my hunch is that they'd have been furious no matter what the reasons. When a spouse has an affair there are always reasons why. But when you are the betrayed spouse no reason is acceptable. In fact, you will probably swat away every reason your husband offers as to why he cheated and tell him it's not good enough. One husband, weary of his failed efforts to explain why he cheated, complained to me, "She doesn't really want an explanation, she wants an execution."

The chapters in this book on communication will help you to have effective conversations with your husband in the aftermath of his infidelity. For now, learning about the key reasons affairs happen can prepare you for those conversations. It's possible to come up with dozens of reasons adultery happens, such as sexual curiosity, boredom, a midlife crisis, loneliness, a need for power or attention, lack of fulfillment, pure happenstance, depression, or retaliation. But the prime factors leading to why your partner cheated fall into one or more of three categories: personal issues and flaws, relationship problems, and life circumstances.

Keep in mind, reasons are not excuses. Reasons point to the factors and the issues that came together in such a way that he ultimately decided to cheat. The more aware you both are of those reasons, the better you can honestly assess your relationship and point yourselves in the direction of change and healing.

Personal Flaws

The infidelity ultimately occurred because your spouse made a choice to cheat. Even if he was unhappy in his life or marriage, he had other options. In the book *Intimacy after Infidelity*, authors Steven Solomon and Lorie Teagno conclude that a person who is unfaithful is fundamentally not dealing with his life effectively. Whether life stresses have become overwhelming, he's unhappy at home, or he simply has an immature "boys will be boys" mentality, infidelity is a destructive way to cope. If your husband views his cheating as wrong and contrary to his own values, he will be more motivated to overcome whatever personal weaknesses contributed to his having been unfaithful. However, some affairs are done purely out of a sense of entitlement, narcissism, and a genuine disregard for the impact the affair will have on others. Those flaws represent long-standing personality characteristics that are difficult to change (since he doesn't view himself as having any problems).

However, there is a huge difference between men who cheat and really don't care at all about the impact of the affair (men with personality disorders) and men who "just didn't think much about it" (the negative consequences of their affair) or were able to pretend that any negative impact would be avoided. In the first case, the man may lack true compassion or empathy. In the second case he does possess compassion and empathy, but through his defense mechanisms was able to kid himself or even completely deny that his actions might result in devastation for you and the family. Men are able to "compartmentalize" more easily than women. They can lock away uncomfortable feelings in a compartment inside their brain and pay less attention to them. So when you ask him, "Didn't you think of me at all when you were meeting with her and going to bed with her?" he may truthfully respond that, no, he barely thought of you while he was with her. Does that represent a total indifference and lack of love? Not necessarily. In fact, if any person with a conscience truly thought about the potentially negative consequences of a hurtful act they were in the middle of committing they would probably halt their actions. But all of us have acted hurtfully, despite having consciences, and regretted it later.

Personal issues might include problems stemming from his childhood. People who had a parent who cheated are more likely themselves to be unfaithful (or marry someone who will be unfaithful). His personal feelings of inadequacy can result in an affair if he starts receiving positive attention from a woman who makes him feel important or worthwhile.

When you are the betrayed spouse, it's common to want to demonize your cheating husband. But the majority of people who have affairs are not bad people. They can be loving and caring people who were unable to deal with their life situations effectively and made extremely poor choices. That means that affairs can actually be a misguided, sometimes unconscious attempt to repair something that's broken or not working in one's life. Most acts of adultery are really efforts to feel loved, accepted, desirable, or worthwhile. That in no way justifies cheating. But if the marriage is to heal it's important to discover what the motivations were underlying your husband's decision to cheat.

Relationship Problems

Your partner will probably point to marital unhappiness as at least part of his reason for cheating. And you may have a great deal of inner conflict about that. On the one hand, you might agree that the marriage wasn't as strong as it could be or even that you hadn't been as attentive or easy to get along with. But on the other hand, you will deeply resent that your husband chose to deal with his dissatisfactions in such a destructive, hurtful way and that he is implying you may be partially to blame. If you refuse to accept that you and the marriage were factors (when he believes they played a role), he will feel you don't understand or care to improve the situation. If you do address marital issues, you may feel you are giving him a "get out of jail free" card and letting him avoid responsibility for his actions.

The solution is not one or the other. It's both. There may have been weaknesses in the relationship (or in you) that contributed *and* he made a clear choice to deal with his unhappiness by having an affair, and he bears the responsibility for that choice. If the two of you are to heal your marriage, each factor must be examined and dealt with. Overlooking one is a mistake. A weak marriage does not cause an affair. There are many couples with weak marriages who remain faithful and many people in happy marriages who cheat. But your marriage is like your immune system. If your immune system is weak you become more susceptible to viruses and infection and you can't bounce back from illness as easily. Since no marriage is perfect it is always a good idea to locate weak spots in your marriage after an affair to improve the odds of recovery and to reduce the odds an affair will happen again.

Your marriage has an increased likelihood of being vulnerable to an affair if any of the following relationship issues exist:

- Very low (or no) sexual desire by one or both partners
- Frequent criticisms, harsh putdowns
- Regular inattentiveness—ships passing in the night
- Emotional detachment; unaware of or disinterested in what is happening with your partner
- Inability to give the benefit of the doubt; judging the other more harshly
- Deep, lingering resentments

In a mature relationship, both partners understand that marriages are not always bliss. But there are some fundamental components that, if missing for any length of time, can force a marriage into a downhill slide.

From the woman's standpoint, it's important not to simply feel loved but to feel beloved—that is, to feel that her husband actually cherishes her. Many men say they love their wives but do not show it in a consistent way that matters to her. If you experience your husband being routinely thoughtless, saying unkind or harsh words, providing go-through-the-motions sex, or having eyes that never seem to light up when he sees you, it can cause you to doubt that his love is very deep. You will then feel inadequate, less desirable, perhaps lonely.

From the man's standpoint, he wants you to feel proud of him, to recognize and appreciate his many sacrifices, and fundamentally to believe in him as someone who is doing his best to provide for and protect his family. He wants respect. He wants you to trust that he loves you even if he doesn't always show it. So when a man hears criticisms, or never sees his wife initiate sex, or feels economic or career pressures that his wife doesn't seem to understand or care about, he feels less cared for, perhaps lonely. Any sense of emotional deprivation by either partner—especially if it continues for a year or more—can increase the odds that an affair might happen.

Life Circumstances

Life circumstances (tragedy, crisis, loss, illness, injury, and so forth) rarely lead to someone having an affair directly. Instead these events are filtered through the marriage and the individual. So a person with a healthy self-esteem, strong coping skills, and a good marriage is more likely to handle the problems life dishes out. On the other hand, when life circumstances become too much to bear and the marriage or individual is emotionally vulnerable, poor choices may be made.

A midlife-crisis affair is one example. Suddenly the person feels his youth is passing him by, his virility may be in question, he becomes anxious that his best years are behind him, and he has an affair to reassure himself he's still "got it." Or a man who is very unhappy with his marriage may decide to end his marriage by having an affair while he is still young enough to enjoy the rest of his life. Those are called "exit affairs" and can happen at any time. An exit affair usually means the marriage is over. The affair didn't cause the marriage to end. The marriage was already ending and the affair became the final nail in the coffin.

Some men have affairs when their wives are pregnant or just gave birth, or when the kids are little. In their minds they feel like a fifth wheel—useless and ignored. But the real problem is that they are insecure and are unable to have effective conversations to address those concerns.

Loss of job or economic standing can be a terrible blow to a man. If he defines himself according to his income or his ability to provide a standard of living to his family, his self-esteem can be crushed. That doesn't automatically mean he will cheat on his wife. But if an opportunity arises combined with an ego that needs soothing, a brief fling or one-night stand might occur. In contrast, a sudden huge rise in economic standing can make some men feel powerful. If they have a weaker value system or if their marriage is already sputtering, their status may allow them more opportunities to have an affair.

Unfortunately, day-to-day life can weigh marriages down resulting in unhappiness, a sense of being rejected or abandoned, and an inclination toward having an affair. Fifty- and sixty-hour work weeks, driving the kids to their various activities, high mortgages, and caring for elderly parents all can result in more conflicts at home or withdrawing from each other. This places the marriage at risk.

Finally, some people have severe emotional disorders that are associated with an increased risk of inappropriate or acting-out behavior. For example, someone with bipolar disorder who is not on a proper level of medications may act out sexually when otherwise they'd never do such a thing.

Often, when an unfaithful spouse has been unhappy or stressed, the affair was a way to stabilize his life. It gave him something to look forward to, to feel good about, or to provide excitement in an otherwise mundane existence. It was an attempt to fix something he felt was broken. If marital problems existed that led to an affair, the affair keeps the marriage from improving. As long as he is involved with another woman in some capacity, the need to repair the marriage is lessened. Whatever loneliness or unhappiness he'd been experiencing at home is compensated for by the other woman. It's only when the affair becomes exposed and is ended that real repairs in the marriage can be made.

The Ultimate Answer

It is highly doubtful that in your conversations with your husband as to why he cheated he will give an answer that makes you respond, "Oh, now I completely understand." You will regard his reasons (and his character) as shabby. But if he is not a philanderer and if your marriage has been at least "good but not great" and yet he still has been unfaithful in some way, the main factors that contributed to his cheating are these: in some ways he did not feel important (either to himself, to the world, or to you), he was unable to talk about it openly or constructively or fix it, and that made him more vulnerable to temptation. Maybe had he never met "her" he never would have cheated. But the main ingredients were in place.

Sometimes the question you keep asking him—"Why did you do this?"—is not really about a search for every possible answer. It's a crying out, an expression of pain, of loss, of grief. It's a way of saying "I can't stand this! Somebody do something! Make it go away!" What must be done in order to make the pain go away is what the rest of this book is about. Noted author and psychologist Gerald Weeks, who coauthored the book *Treating Infidelity*, pointed out that perhaps in the final analysis "infidelity . . . cannot be explained. It can only be forgiven."

Forgiveness is hard. Often, before forgiveness can happen, other things must happen first. That's what the next several chapters are about.

first things first: immediate actions to take (and avoid)

Imagine arriving home and discovering that your house has been thoroughly ransacked and everything is in shambles. It isn't simply a matter of calling the police and cleaning up. Now you feel afraid to be in your own home and to sleep in your bed at night. *Who did this? Why? Will they do it again? Will I ever feel safe?* As you look at the destruction around you, you wonder, *Where do I even begin to get my life back in order?*

After an affair has been exposed, your life—your emotional life and your everyday, practical life (job, responsibilities, and so forth)— is in such disarray you don't know what to do first. The most typical response is to become paralyzed or to act out impulsively. You will probably regret later any rash action you take now. Yes, there are things to do immediately. But part of you is in shock and not thinking clearly. Fear and anger is justifiable but it interferes with sound judgment. Your husband allowed his feelings to run his life and affect his decision to be unfaithful. Admit your feelings, discover their message, but don't allow them to manipulate you like a puppet on a string. Your husband wasn't smart. Be smarter than him.

Halt! Don't Go There! (At Least Not at the Moment)

In the immediate hours and days after an affair has been exposed, the hurt partner is tempted to act in one or more of seven counterproductive ways. None of these ways are smart, unless the affair was "the final straw" and you are absolutely certain the marriage is now over. Even then, you may create more problems for yourself.

Number 1: Don't Threaten Divorce or Separation

Yelling, "Get out! It's over!" rarely helps (other than perhaps making you feel powerful). A more honest and less messy (for you) response might be, "I don't know if I can stay in this marriage or not. I need time to think and to see what happens." You still may not even be sure what your partner wants to do. If he is leaning toward leaving you for "her," kicking him out may make his decision easy. If he wants the marriage to survive, he may refuse to leave. That could either infuriate you or ease your mind. Or he might believe that you sincerely want the marriage to end and he may not even try to save it, believing his actions are unforgivable. One man came to my office for his initial session, convinced his marriage was finished after his affair. He hated the idea of losing his wife but she was adamant that it was impossible to repair. A month later she changed her mind and concluded he must not have really cared about her because he gave up so quickly.

A brief separation has drawbacks. If you need time to think or just not see his face and want to punish him, insisting he stay somewhere else for a short while may give you some time to sort things out. But if his mistress still poses a threat, can you handle the idea that he might be seeing more of her now that he isn't living with you?

Number 2: Don't Tell Your Family

As time goes on you might decide to tell your parents or siblings about the affair (or they may catch on that something is wrong). But if you and your husband reconcile, will there be bad blood between him and your family? You might think: *So what? If the price he has to pay for cheating on me is to be uncomfortable around my family then so be it.* Perhaps. But it might mean that family get-togethers from now on will be awkward and uncomfortable for everyone, not just him. Your family is not objective. What if your parents insist that you must stay married no matter what? You might think they don't understand you and you will have lost some of your closeness with them. Or they might demonize your husband. But what if you decide to reconcile? They might be upset with you for not heeding their advice. Furthermore, if your family has had its own set of problems, your issue may stir the pot. What if your sister and your mother argue with each other about what you should do? What if your dad cheated on your mother years ago?

If you decide to end the marriage, by all means tell your family if it will gain you some support. Otherwise, delay that option as long as possible. Similarly, be selective about which friends you might choose to talk to. If they are close to your husband, they may feel uncomfortable getting in the middle or may take sides. Later on, you may find some of those friendships damaged. If you need to talk to someone, choose a friend who is not closely connected to your husband or speak to a therapist or trusted member of the clergy. If you do tell family and close friends, be careful not to give them daily updates during the roller coaster phase. Again, they are not objective and they are human. Chances are they will become a bit exasperated and offer advice you vehemently disagree with, or they may grow tired of dropping everything to hear your story, which will create even more emotional pain and confusion for you.

Number 3: Don't Tell the Kids

They can do nothing about the situation. It will only make them anxious and upset. And they may feel obligated to take sides. They might feel betrayed as well. There is enough emotional pain that must be healed; don't add the children's pain to that list. If the affair was an exit affair, then it was not the reason the marriage ended. There is no need to mention it to the children. (If you feel a need, it's born of vengeance. Vengeance is not a good motive.) If he plans on staying with the other woman, the kids will know soon enough.

Number 4: Don't Undermine His Job

Maybe you know many of his coworkers and would like nothing more than to make them aware of what he did. Or maybe his job would be directly affected by his actions (he's not supposed to have a relationship with a coworker; he used company time to send her e-mails, and so forth). One betrayed wife knew that her husband's boss went through a painful divorce from a philandering husband. She called the woman and told her, "If you notice that Jim looks preoccupied at work, it's because our marriage is on the rocks after I discovered he'd been cheating on me." The boss spoke to the husband, who felt thoroughly undermined by his wife; their efforts to rebuild the marriage screeched to a halt.

If your husband is having (or just ended) an affair with a coworker, he will resent you if he or his mistress gets fired or transferred because you spilled the beans. If he still has feelings for the other woman, your actions may bring them closer together.

Number 5: Don't Make Unrealistic Demands

He owes you. Big time. If he is sincerely remorseful and truly wants to remain married, he will cooperate with many of your demands and requests. There is no need to make requests that break his back. For example, insisting he quit his job to get away from "her" may be unrealistic. Or insisting you relocate out of state may be equally difficult. You must ask yourself if the "solutions" will create more problems than they solve.

Demands that restrict his freedoms may be helpful temporarily. But over time they must be relaxed if trust is to grow. For example, you might insist he allow you to check his cell phone, e-mails, and voice messages. Fine. If he used to go out for a drink after work on a Friday with coworkers (and "she" was there) he will need to stop that. Fine. Telling him he can no longer go on business trips when his job requires that is unrealistic. He might be able to skip a trip or two, or delay one, but that's it.

Waking him up at two A.M. and insisting he answer questions might be tolerable at first, but he will quickly resist. Avoid this line of reasoning: *If you really loved me and wanted our marriage to work you would do what I ask.* That's emotional blackmail. He may indeed want the marriage to work but may decide it will be impossible for it to work given all of the unrealistic demands.

Number 6: Don't Show Your Hand

If you have additional information about his affair that he doesn't know you know, keep it to yourself. It may help you later when you ask him questions that you already know the answer to. If he answers truthfully, you might feel more confident that he is truthful in general. Certainly, if he is at risk for continuing his affair or if a legal separation or divorce may happen, be smart about when to divulge what you know. If you tell him you've programmed the computer to store all of his e-mails in a folder only you can retrieve, he'll stop sending e-mails to his girlfriend. But you won't know if he stopped because he ended the affair or if he's just being clever.

Number 7: Don't Degrade or Lower Yourself

When a major crisis has passed and people are somewhat trauma-tized, they often later review what happened and are disturbed by their own actions that occurred at the beginning of the crisis. You don't want to lose sleep at night thinking *I can't believe I actually did that*. Such actions might include having a revenge affair, flirting with other men, or embarrassing or humiliating him in public.

What's the difference between intuition and paranoia?

Any knee-jerk reaction you have that is accompanied by strong feelings of fear or rage is likely due to your mistrust of your partner, but it is not necessarily accurate. For example, if he's running late and you automatically think "He's with *her!*" and you feel strong emotions, there's a greater chance you are over-reacting. Genuine intuition is less emotionally fueled. It comes about as a kind of quiet knowing, unaccompanied by intense waves of emotion.

Drinking heavily, acts of violence against your spouse (or his prop-erty), or having a "revenge affair" may only make you feel worse about yourself. Hasn't your self-esteem taken a big enough hit already?

Similarly, blaming yourself for his affair isn't a good idea. Take ownership for whatever flaws you have that contributed to marital problems, but don't accept responsibility for his choices. One betrayed wife called up the other woman at her job and made threats. She never intended to carry out the threats but hoped to intimidate her husband's mistress. Instead she was arrested. Begging your husband to stay with you isn't smart. If he comes back he will feel as if he has the upper hand, that he did you a favor by remaining in the marriage, and will probably tell you to "get over it" (his affair) without trying to really work through repairing the marriage. You won't feel secure.

There are some steps you should probably take fairly soon. They might be uncomfortable but they will reduce anxiety in the long run.

1. **Get tested for an STD.** Go to a physician you don't know if you're embarrassed to see your regular doctor. Also, don't even think about having sex with him until he too gets tested. He may insist his affair wasn't sexual or that he used a condom if it was. But his veracity is in question right now. Don't lose sleep. Get tested.

2. **Know your rights.** Talk to an attorney or read a book on the laws in your state. It doesn't mean you're planning for a divorce, but it's helpful to know what to expect financially and what might transpire legally if you go that route. Be informed.

3. **Remind yourself that all of this is temporary.** It's hell now but it won't be this way forever. If you both want your marriage to survive and are willing to work to make that happen, you will feel significantly better six months from now. In a year you'll feel even

better. Even if matters don't work out the way you want you will adjust. Your emotions will get under control and you will learn to be okay with your new lifestyle. Your life is far from over.

4. **Talk to someone you trust but use good judgment.** Don't talk to too many people. Otherwise you'll exhaust yourself giving updates over and over. The best person is someone who cares but has objectivity.

Decisions to Make
(Despite Your Mixed Emotions)

Since your emotions and the current status of your marriage are in flux, you might find it hard to make any hard-and-fast decisions right now. And any decision you make today may not last. However, it's important that as soon as possible you make a decision whether to invest time and energy working on your marriage (to see if it can be saved) or to decide not to work on it. The decision to work on it is not only yours to make. If your spouse doesn't want any part of it, you will have no choice but to prepare for the end of your marriage.

Indecision is common but it's really a decision to *not* work on the marriage. Indecision results in haphazard, in-flux, always-confusing actions that will make the marriage boat slowly sink, not remain afloat. You will take two steps forward and two backward. Over time both of you will be highly discouraged and will lose your energy and motivation to persevere.

If we assume for now that your husband has not made a clear decision to be with the other woman, your decision to hang in there will be based upon your answer to two questions: whether or not the marriage has a fair chance of surviving, and whether or not you can handle the long process of recovery or divorce.

Can This Marriage Be Saved?

Some factors increase the odds that a marriage can recover from an affair, and some factors lower the odds. Don't make a snap decision. And you need to be able to live with uncertainty. No matter what you choose, you can't be certain it is for the best. All outcomes must play out over time.

Is He Willing to Stop the Affair and All (Reasonable) Contact with the Other Woman?

Until he does, there is no way that the marriage can improve and recovery from the betrayal can occur. The problem is that if he had feelings for her, he may claim he wants to end the affair but finds it hard to do so. Or he may feel a deep need to connect with her periodically just to find out how she's doing. Or she may be unwilling to end it and finds ways to contact him repeatedly, even though he does not wish to see or speak to her. In my experience, when a spouse had romantic feelings for an affair partner and tries to end that relationship, it is rarely done neatly, in a "once and for all" manner. Instead the "couple" still manages to contact each other and at best wean from their relationship. During this time, his thoughts of her will intensify; he will miss her. That will cause him some confusion as to what he really wants. If this leads to a regular resumption of their affair, the marriage is seriously threatened. It is better for you to understand that once he ends his affair he will still have feelings for her and may contact her for a while even after he says he stopped. That is far from ideal and will absolutely reduce your faith in him. However, it may be unrealistic to expect that he'll be able to cut her off completely. It's best if he can. If he cannot, it doesn't automatically mean he is unwilling to make his marriage work. But no progress will be made until he does.

Does He Take Responsibility for His Actions?

If he blames you for his affair and refuses to admit that it was his choice and no one made him do it, you will not have a satisfying marriage. He's not capable of having a mature relationship. He's not blaming you if he points to aspects of the marriage that made him unhappy. He may be realistically examining the factors that led to his cheating. But he must be able to admit that his decision to have an affair, despite whatever unhappiness he was experiencing, was his alone.

Is He Remorseful?

Does he believe that what he did was wrong? Does he feel badly that he hurt you? Or does he say, "Yes, I hurt you but . . ." and then try to justify his actions? Does he expect you to "get over it" quickly? Is he impatient and defensive when you ask him questions about his day? Does he expect you to warm up to him and complain that you're "dredging up the past" when you are still clearly distraught over his cheating? Then he has little compassion or understanding of what you are going through. Does he say, "What's the big deal?" If so, he doesn't get it. If he has no remorse and does not accept responsibility for his actions, he likely has a personality disorder (antisocial personality or narcissistic personality) and the marriage will never be healthy.

Is He Willing to Restrict His Lifestyle for at Least Several Months to Give You Time to Regain Trust?

It's no fun being his probation officer but that's how it might have to be for a while. He must be willing to submit to questions and to have you doubt his truthfulness (even when he's being truthful). He must give up hobbies or interests that you consider risky and must be willing to have no privacy regarding his e-mails or phone calls. He might need to turn over some joint-account money to you so that you will have funds on hand in case you need to retain a lawyer, hire a private investigator, or pay for rent in an apartment. These restrictions must come to an end at some point, but that should happen over time as trust builds—not because he is offended by it. If he is sincerely remorseful he will care more about your ability to feel more trusting than on giving up some of his freedoms and tolerating a few minor indignities.

Is He Willing to Rebuild the Marriage and Himself?

Many unfaithful spouses hope that the marriage will recover primarily through the passage of time and the ending of the affair. They may try to be on their best behavior but they view recovery as similar to recovering from a broken leg—just don't do any more damage to it and it will heal. That isn't enough. Certainly, if there were marital problems before the affair those problems must be addressed. But he may also need to gain insight into himself. Reading books on the subject or having some sessions with a therapist may help him gain insight. He may want to get past what happened by viewing it as "over and done with" and may be loath to analyze his actions in any depth. Since one of your concerns is reducing the odds infidelity could ever happen again, you'll probably feel better knowing he's doing his best to examine why he did what he did and, if possible, learn what he can do to improve himself.

Can You Cope?

No matter what you decide—end the marriage or stick with it—you will be challenged. It's beyond the scope of this book to address all of the issues you might face if you choose to get a divorce. Not only will it cost you financially, but you may have to move out or decide on custody arrangements if you have children. You'd have to struggle to be an effective coparent with someone you no longer respect. If he is with his mistress (or finds another mate) you may have to contend with jealousy issues or with worrying if she will be a good stepparent to your children. You will cope better if you have a good support system of friends and family. Many couples who might choose to divorce decide instead to give the marriage another try because they have children or because they simply cannot afford to live apart. Those are legitimate reasons to make sure you've done all you can to save the marriage before ending it.

Can You Tolerate Not Knowing for Sure?

If you need to have outcomes all figured out before you make a decision, you will have a hard time now. No matter what you decide, the outcome is not entirely in your hands. You could sincerely try to make the marriage work only to discover that your husband still chooses her over you six months down the road. Or you could catch him in more lies. Or he could cheat again and leave you feeling like a complete fool. You must be willing to risk such outcomes if you choose to work on the marriage. You can't hold back a bit from giving it your all—to protect yourself in case the bottom falls out—because the bottom might fall out of your marriage precisely because you didn't give it your all.

Can You Live with the Inevitable Ups and Downs?

Chances are at least one of you has strong mixed feelings. Maybe he isn't sure that he wants to stay married, or maybe you're the one who can't decide. Maybe you're not sure you can ever forgive him or trust him again. Normal, happy marriages have ups and downs. Those ups and downs are magnified in the months following an infidelity. You have to be willing to approach it as you might the stock market. The market goes up and down every day. If you hope to remain in the market for the long run it's best to ignore daily fluctuations and look for overall trends. If your marriage is improving (or failing) over time, that may be a better indicator than what happens on any given day.

Can You Look Inward?

The focus can't be all on what he does. He also will be reacting to you as you try to rebuild. Make sure you are aware of your impact on him. It's good for each of you to ask "What's it like for him (her) to have me around right now?" If the answer is not very flattering you must be willing to make some changes. That doesn't mean you aren't entitled to be angry or hard to get along with. In the immediate aftermath of an affair you may have a difficult time being calm and reasonable. But if you decide to rebuild the marriage, then over time you will have less justification to be angry, standoffish, vengeful, cold, or otherwise uncooperative. You'll have to put aside anger for the larger goal of healing the marriage.

Looking inward also means examining old wounds. For example, if you felt abandoned by a parent, that issue will get stirred up as you cope with your husband's affair. If you decide to divorce, long-standing insecurities also can resurface, such as feelings of inadequacy or an inability to cope with loneliness. That's another reason why speaking to a trained professional might help.

One of the hardest things to accomplish after a spouse has been unfaithful is to be able to accept that reality on an emotional level. Anger, fear, shock, and denial keep you fighting against the reality of what happened. The next chapter is crucial in helping you to recover emotionally and put yourself in the best position to deal effectively with whatever your future brings.

emotional acceptance: the most powerful thing you can achieve

In the early weeks and even months after an infidelity has been exposed, you will experience a maelstrom of emotions, often played out simultaneously—hurt, rage, guilt, depression, and fear. It's confusing at best, exhausting certainly, and even physically debilitating the longer your future remains in limbo. A simple clue that you are far from regaining any emotional control over yourself is the number of unending questions you have spinning in your head. The more uncertain you are of what will happen in the future, and the less sense you can make of all that has happened so far, the more obsessed you will be and the more pain you will feel. The pain of betrayal is experienced as a form of grief. And the prospect of future grief (an inability to heal the marriage or your heart) is experienced as fear or despair.

Do you feel like crawling into a hole right now and closing off the world? Do you feel like lashing out? Do you find it hard to get through your head what your husband did? Then the enormity of what has happened has not yet integrated into your psyche. You're still in high-reactive mode. Many people get stuck there for longer than necessary.

This chapter reveals how to be less emotionally reactive so that you can make better decisions and act in ways that will serve you, not make matters worse. You will discover a simple but powerful way to dramatically reduce the awful mind-chatter and put at ease the many worrisome thoughts that keep you awake at night and preoccupied during the day. To your amazement, you will discover that achieving this greater calmness has nothing to do with getting answers to your many questions or to resolving any of the uncertainties that now plague you. In fact, part of the reason for your anguish is that you seek answers to questions that, at least for now, cannot be answered with any degree of certainty (*"Will my marriage survive? Can I ever love or trust him again? Can I make it on my own? Will I find someone else who loves me? Will my children be okay no matter what happens? What's the real reason he cheated?"*). You look for certainty when no certainty is possible. You must cultivate trust when you have reason to mistrust; faith when you have reason to disbelieve; and hope when you have reason to despair. And to accomplish all of that you must first and foremost *emotionally accept* what has happened when you find it completely unacceptable.

Emotional acceptance is key—I can't overstate that.

Everyone who copes well in the aftermath of an affair and is able to *really* put their lives back together has achieved emotional acceptance. However, they were probably unaware of that fact or downplayed it—and were unable to take full advantage of it. Wouldn't it be nice to truly understand what will be at the basis of your emotional healing and take steps now to help bring that about rather than stagger along?

Read this chapter carefully. Chances are you will resist the concept of emotional acceptance because you do not fully understand its meaning or its power. In fact, a part of your brain has been programmed to resist it (*"What he did was unacceptable!"*). Another part of your brain has been programmed to embrace the concept of emotional acceptance, but that part is less dominant and easily overpowered during times of crisis. Correcting that imbalance is what this chapter is about.

In fact, the more you find yourself resisting the idea of emotionally accepting what has happened, the more you absolutely need it.

What Is Emotional Acceptance?

Emotional acceptance is the ability to stop fighting, stop resisting—on an emotional level—the reality of what has happened. It is the shift from *"How could this happen!"* to *"I accept that it happened even though it is devastating. Now I must figure out what to do."* It is the ability to be less emotionally reactive during a crazy, heart-wrenching time. It is going from *"This can't be!"* to *"It is"* without the searing pain and drama.

You might understand it better when you realize what it isn't. Emotional acceptance is not:

Passivity. By accepting the situation you do not sit back and do nothing. You must take action to cope, heal your wounds, and move forward with confidence. But if you resist certain realities (*"It should never have happened in the first place!"*) you only slow down your progress or bang your head against a wall.

Tolerance. You can be morally against what happened as long as you emotionally accept the reality that it did indeed happen. Tolerance happens when we "put up with" something we don't like.

Rewarding bad behavior. You might worry that if you accept your husband's infidelity you are treating what he did as a misdemeanor and letting him off the hook with a slap on the wrist and a month of probation. To be emotionally accepting does not stop you from making his life difficult. There will be many times you will be enraged, cold, accusatory, and punitive. That's standard fare in most marriages after a serious betrayal. But when you emotionally come to terms with what happened you will not prolong your own misery.

Minimizing what was done. In fact, to fully emotionally accept what has happened you must see it fully for what it was and not make molehills out of mountains. Denial, pretending, and making excuses has no place when it comes to emotional acceptance.

When you are in a state of emotional acceptance you are aligned with reality. Then you see it for what it is and are better able to decide what needs to happen next.

Think for a moment about someone who lost a loved one and was in deep grief. Chances are as time passed that person was able to resume a life where the pain of loss no longer got in the way. He may always miss the loved one who died, yet his life no longer feels hopeless or empty. What happened? He was able to fully accept and embrace on an emotional level what happened. You will more than likely arrive at that place some day. But you can get there sooner and with less emotional upheaval once you accept what happened rather than resist the reality of it.

It's a Brain Thing

The more you are suffering right now, the more the left side (the fighter, the analyzer, the worrier, the problem-finder, and the solution-seeker) of your brain is dominating the right side. To cope as well as can be expected, both sides need to be balanced. But under stress the majority of people automatically (with no awareness of doing so) switch into left-brain-dominant mode—as a way to reduce their stress—only to find themselves more stressed than ever before.

The left brain keeps asking questions and demands answers. Even when some answers are found, inner peace gets pushed aside by the left brain's persistent need to scan for more problems and search for more or better solutions. *There is no easing of the mind in the left brain, no calmness, only worry and agitation.* Every time you are obsessed with questions and worry about "Who? . . . Why? . . . When? . . . What if?" it's the left side of your brain that's in full swing. And you may see nothing wrong with that because you believe that better answers are "out there" and that it's a good idea to anticipate what else could go wrong so you can prevent it or better protect yourself. The left side of your brain operates best when problems can be understood clearly and solutions are all in place. For example, if your tire goes flat you can decide to fix it or to call someone to fix it. It might be a hassle but the solution is there. But many of life's real problems don't have immediate answers. If you are diagnosed with a life-threatening illness you can receive treatment but there are no guarantees it will help. There are no solutions, just decisions to make along the way that will give you feedback as to what to do next. Often, the ultimate answers are out of your hands. Similarly, worries about money, relationships, the welfare of your children, and so forth do not have permanent solutions (you may always worry about your children's welfare even when they're adults). The left side of your brain doesn't handle those issues easily. It wants answers. It doesn't like to manage problems over time but eradicate them. Under severe threat (physical or psychological) your left brain is uneasy with the idea of "Let's wait and see what happens."

Peace of mind comes about by having access to the right side of your brain. The right side of your brain doesn't examine details. Instead it tries to see the whole picture. The right brain has a "go with the flow" philosophy. It doesn't resist your efforts to change what you can change or to anticipate problems ahead but it wants you to stop trying to fix what cannot, at least for now, be fixed. When you have an important goal, you want to be sure that your efforts will pay off. Your right brain knows that some efforts cannot guarantee results because other factors (situations, people) come into play that you have no control over. It wants you to "cross bridges when you get there" when circumstances cannot always be predicted ahead of time. People who cope well don't need to have a crystal ball. They have a confidence that they can respond to a changing situation and will reassess things as they go along. Backup plans are fine but only go so far. The right brain accepts the situation at the moment. Not because it's good or desirable but because it is. Therefore, a person who manages adversity well *accepts* that something unwanted has happened (a right-brain response), analyzes the situation and makes changes where possible (a left-brain response), and then *accepts* it when there is no more they can do at that time (a right-brain response). If the left brain dominates, the person will refuse to emotionally accept the situation at that moment ("I can't believe this happened!") and will always be on edge, like a suspicious prison guard, unable to relax, unable to trust, always searching for what can go wrong.

The right brain allows for creative solutions. Many "ah-ha!" moments happen out of the blue, without intense thinking. Any overdone, obsessive thinking and worrying (a left-brain response) chokes off access to the right side of the brain. In fact, when you are in a state of emotional crisis, you will go into fight-or-flight mode and *not* think creatively. (Imagine you are at a circus and a ferocious tiger escapes from its cage. Panicked, you will probably run for your life, and I guarantee you will not think creatively.) That is why people in careers that might involve sudden, life-threatening situations (emergency room staff, pilots, air-traffic controllers, police and military personnel, and so on) have to practice coping with such emergencies under supervised conditions until they learn to manage their fear so as to be able to think clearly and to come up with creative solutions if need be.

If your partner had a recent affair you will likely be panicked and in shock—a state of "fight or flee"—and your thinking is limited. Creative solutions are then impossible to come by, as is the ability to put the affair into any useful perspective. Your thinking is black or white, love or hate, trust or mistrust, fury or fear, leave or stay. In order to access creative thought and in order to access the part of the brain (the right hemisphere) that promotes well-being, acceptance, and trust, you must lower your vigilance from time to time and endeavor to accept what happened, not emotionally resist it.

Emotional Acceptance Versus Emotional Resistance

I mentioned earlier that one clue to the fact that you are not in a state of emotional acceptance is when your mind is flooded by neverending questions. A second clue is when you find yourself doing battle with *yourself*—not just your husband. You think one way, then immediately challenge yourself and think another way, but no resolution is reached. In other words, this entire situation has stirred you up with doubts and uncertainties and you wage a war within yourself trying to arrive at an acceptable understanding of what happened, why it happened, what it means for your life, and what to do about it. The internal battle may look something like this:

"I'll never trust him . . . But I want to!"

"It must be my fault . . . No it's entirely his fault!"

"I want to leave him . . . But I still love him!"

"I want to call that woman's husband and ruin her life! . . . No, I want to leave her alone and focus on my relationship."

"He doesn't deserve me . . . But we had a good thing going once."

"No one else will want me . . . No, I'm an attractive and desirable person."

A third clue that you are not yet fully accepting what happened is that you engage in black-and-white thinking—a defense mechanism. But that thinking style squeezes complicated issues into two categories—which means that no matter what you do it's probably not a decision that takes into account all options. Affairs don't have snappy solutions that fall into place easily for everyone.

A fourth clue to the lack of emotional acceptance is using "should" thinking. Any time you find yourself using the words "should" or "shouldn't" you are stepping back from the harsh reality of what happened. *"He should never have betrayed me . . . I should leave him . . .*

I should forgive him . . ." and similar lines of thought usually have the effect of squashing emotional acceptance in favor of emotional resistance. It forces you to argue with reality or with yourself. That's because "should" thinking doesn't always stem from a balanced perspective but comes from a reliance on standby philosophies or concerns about what other people might think that may not be useful for your situation. (So many women I've counseled had told me they always believed they'd never stay with a man who cheated. And yet now that their husbands have done so, the women aren't clear about what to do. "Should" thinking is easy to apply when you are not the one in the middle of the crisis.)

How to Become More Emotionally Accepting

Imagine thinking "He betrayed me so I should leave him." What are you really saying? If by saying that you mean, "I want to leave him and I intend to leave him and I have no concerns about doing so" then there is no resistance to your beliefs (inner reality). But chances are after you say "I should leave him" your next thoughts may be "But I can't afford it . . . he deserves another chance . . . it's against my religious faith to leave . . . I still love him . . ." Now you are in conflict.

Until now you chose to deal with that conflict by arguing with yourself (or others) about what to do. Arguing and debating creates tension and is the opposite of emotional acceptance. What if you accepted your entire inner reality—which includes contradictory beliefs—and said, "I should leave him *and* I don't want to leave him," and left it at that? There is no war. You are not debating yourself or forcing yourself to make a decision. You are merely accepting that at this moment in time you are of two minds. You went from "either-or" thinking to "both-and" thinking. "Both-and" thinking happens when you *accept* that the situation has no clear-cut answers—at least not now. It means you are willing to live with uncertainty and stop asking questions that cannot be answered right now. By halting the either-or thinking and by accepting that your feelings are mixed, you stop resisting the reality of the moment (the reality of your ambivalence) and are able to breathe a little easier and focus on the truth of all of your feelings, not just half of them. You stop looking for answers you cannot find right now and accept the uncertainty of things. To do otherwise is to resist reality, to fight what you cannot change or figure out, and to repeatedly ask questions that have no clear answers. I can hear you asking, "Shouldn't I come up with answers? Who wants to remain in a state of uncertainty?" If answers were readily forthcoming you'd have had them in your pocket by now. If you decide to stay or leave, trust him or not, forgive him or hold him in contempt, you will always have uncertainty. How do you live with uncertainty without going batty? By accepting it.

As a simple test, imagine that you cannot trust your husband but want to be able to. Say the words "I don't trust him" and notice the tension you feel in your body (likely in your stomach, chest, or throat area). Now say the words "But I want to trust him" and again notice the tension. I'm betting that your tension level stayed the same. It created tension to say, "I don't trust him" because a part of you is fighting that idea and dearly wishes you could trust him.

Similarly, it created tension to say, "I want to trust him" because you know that right now you cannot. In other words, you created or sustained inner tension by artificially trying to talk yourself into some belief that for now is only partially true. Now, as you remain aware of your physical tension, repeat the phrase "I accept that I don't trust him." How does that feel? Now say, "And I accept that I want to trust him." Repeat it again, this time as a single sentence: "I accept that I don't trust him and I accept that I want to trust him." Many of you trying this will have noticed a reduction in physical tension. Why? Because you stopped resisting the true reality of how you feel—which is mixed and somewhat contradictory. You were willing to accept uncertainty because that is the true state of the situation at the moment. You were aligned with reality rather than opposed to it.

If instead you continued to feel a lot of tension with no reduction, all that means is that there is more to the story that you have yet to accept that must be articulated. For example, your line of thinking might continue in this fashion:

- But if I trust him he may hurt me again. (So say: *I accept that if I trust him he may hurt me again.*)
- I refuse to be hurt again. (*I accept that I refuse to be hurt again.*)
- But the only way to guarantee this is to end the marriage and I'm not sure I want to do that. (*I accept that the only way to guarantee this is to end the marriage and I accept that I don't want to do that.*)
- This is so unfair! (*I accept that this is so unfair.*)
- I'm so furious! (*I accept that I'm so furious.*)

- But I'm tired of being angry, tired of all the yelling. (*I accept that I'm tired of being angry. I accept that I'm tired of all the yelling.*)
- I just want to be able to believe in him again. (*I accept that I want to be able to believe in him again.*)

That inner talk with yourself could go on and on for pages. The point is for you to accept every thought and feeling as it emerges, even if it contradicts previous thoughts, and stop the inner battle. You can't beat up one thought with another and come away feeling rested and hopeful. So when a woman who has been betrayed exclaims to me, "I don't know if I want him in my life or out of my life!" I ask her simply to repeat to herself, *"I accept that I want him in my life and I accept that I want him out of my life. Both are true for me right at this moment. I accept that both are true. I accept that answers will come in time and I accept that I wish I had answers now . . ."*

The result? She feels calmer, less agitated, because she has stopped the inner battle. Her inner mixed feelings now peacefully coexist with each other.

The next chapter is one of several that will help you understand which of your thoughts are helpful and which are unhelpful to your goal of healing the wounds in your marriage and moving on with your life.

it's all in your head: ideas to embrace and ideas to erase

Whether you are headed for divorce, trying to reconcile, or stuck somewhere in between, you are probably holding on to certain counterproductive beliefs. Those beliefs are as true to you as the belief that the earth is round. And you believe that to let go of certain beliefs is a kind of death. In fact, it is. It is the death of your ego—your identity. You regard yourself as being a person who holds dear certain "truths" or "principles." To change those core beliefs is to change who you are. It would be like changing your religion or discovering that the people who raised you were in fact not your biological parents. Your whole sense of who you are would be uprooted. You are probably working hard to make your marriage can survive and your heart heal, yet at the same time you've latched on to a set of beliefs that are completely incompatible with that goal. For example, you may wholeheartedly believe "He cheated so he must not truly love me. All of his words have been lies." At the same time you want to save the relationship and find ways for the two of you to be happy again. Do you understand how much harder it is to have faith in your future together while believing that he must not have loved you in the first place? If you hope to stay in the marriage and be happy again, you'll have to loosen up your hold on certain beliefs.

Beliefs That Keep You Stuck

Your unhelpful beliefs tend to fall into two categories: those that are probably true (more or less) but that you refuse to accept; and those that are probably untrue but that you refuse to abandon. Thus, every time you latch on to one of those beliefs you have no option but to get frustrated, bang your head against a wall, and create more (and unnecessary) pain for yourself. And if your spouse disagrees with your beliefs ("Even though I cheated on you I still love you!") it only sets the two of you up to debate and argue. Neither of you will feel understood and both of you will start to feel hopeless that matters can be resolved.

Is It Really Him You're Arguing With?

Sometimes we express a strong belief such as "There is no excuse for having an affair" but then may inwardly argue with ourselves about the truthfulness of that belief ("But can I be sure that's true?"). Since being of two minds causes tremendous discomfort when the issue is of great consequence, it is a common human reaction to prefer to argue with others than with ourselves. Therefore you may find yourself debating your spouse when he takes an opposing position when in reality you are trying to avoid debating yourself.

Ideas to Embrace

If you took the time to write down all of the ideas you cannot fully accept about your situation but that your husband (or others) want you to accept, you could end up with a long list. Every time you chip away at a belief it may seem as if you are not standing your ground. That will make you resist making an honest appraisal of the situation. Truth is often found in the gray areas. It's very rarely possible to pigeonhole people as all good or all bad. Good people can make bad choices and bad people can make good choices. When it comes to complicated situations, life is never open and shut. Consider the following five beliefs that, if you embrace them, can make your effort to get past the hurt and betrayal easier.

The Fact That He Betrayed You Doesn't Necessarily Mean He Doesn't Love You

If he says he still loves you he may be telling the truth. Hurting people you love is not a new phenomenon. If he loves you, his cheating says more about his inability to deal with his unhappiness, his impulses, or his emotional needs in a constructive way. As long as you claim "If you loved me you wouldn't have cheated" you have no other conclusion to draw other than he doesn't love you. But is that really true? Look deep in your heart at the totality of who he is. Do you really believe he has no love for you? If you cannot believe he loves you when he insists he still does, you have reason to doubt him. After all, he's lied before. But for now it's best to accept both sides of the issue. *I accept that I believe he must not love me if he cheated, and I accept that it's possible he still loves me.* You don't need to make a final decision on the truth of his love. If he wants to make the marriage work and you wish that it could work, you must go with the flow (a right-brain response) until more accurate information comes your way in time.

He May Have Lied but That Doesn't Necessarily Make Him a Liar

Infidelity and lying go hand in hand. They're a package deal. At first it is a lie of omission—not telling you what he's been doing.

Then if your suspicions are aroused he will lie to prevent getting caught. Lies soon build upon one another as he must continue to lie in order to not reveal that his previous statements also were lies. And once the truth of the affair is out in the open he may still lie because he fears making the situation worse by telling you more details of the truth. Or he will lie when he denies he was in contact with "her" after he strongly claimed he'd never speak to her again. (To be honest, everybody lies. Researchers claim that in an average ten-minute conversation with friends a person will lie up to three times. Usually the lies are done to enhance self-esteem or to avoid hurting someone's feelings.) If your husband was a fairly honest guy before his affair, and he wants to be trusted by you again, you're better off viewing him as someone capable of lying under certain conditions but not completely label him as a liar. If you are unsure about that, ask yourself: Have I ever lied after having done something I was ashamed of or didn't want others to know about? If so, does that make me a liar or a person who has lied and who has also spoken the truth?

He May Regret He Hurt You, but Not Regret the Affair

Unless he had an affair to purposely exit the marriage or to be vengeful, most affairs are not committed for the purpose of hurting a spouse or the children. If he had feelings for the other woman—even a little bit—he may still regard some aspects of the affair positively, even though he feels badly that you were hurt. If he does have some positive feelings about his affair, you will probably feel threatened by that. You may worry he will want to return to her. Keep in mind that no one continues an affair unless there is something worthwhile about it. But even when aspects of the affair are worthwhile, people can end affairs and remain faithful to their spouses afterward.

Similarly, he may have fond memories of the affair after it has ended. If you keep asking him about that and he admits it, you can choose to view that as a threat to your marriage or as an understandable (but somewhat unpleasant for you) consequence of many affairs. Again, if you are honest with yourself, you may fondly recall many parts of your earlier life (before you met your husband) and even fantasize about those things—and that doesn't necessarily mean you wish you weren't married. If your husband sincerely regrets how he hurt you and has taken clear and persistent steps to prove to you his devotion and commitment to the marriage, it is best to accept that any positive memories he has of his affair are memories only, and not a threat to you.

You May Never Know the Whole Truth

Getting to the heart of the matter seems like a sensible thing. Why did he do it? And has he told you *everything*? The trouble is when you ask him certain questions he will likely respond, "I don't remember" or "I don't know." It will look like he's being evasive. And that may or may not be the case. If he is being evasive to hide the fact that he is still carrying on with the other woman, you will eventually find that out. Some men are evasive because revealing additional details will only inflame the situation and they hope to focus on rebuilding things instead. For example, some men will refuse to describe their sexual activities with the other woman in any graphic detail. One husband told me in private that he had taken his mistress to a vacation spot that was one of his wife's favorites because he was familiar with the area. He also never told his mistress that he and his wife vacationed there many times. When his wife pressed him for details about his weekend trips with "her," he lied about where he'd gone knowing it would devastate his wife if she knew the truth.

If he isn't consciously hiding aspects of the truth he still may not be that insightful. "I don't know" may be an honest answer. He never thought out why he was having an affair and never thought through the implications should he get caught.

Sometimes, more parts of the truth come out in bits and pieces over time. That's because as the marriage improves and trust is being restored, his anxiety and defenses will be reduced and he may suddenly have more insights or believe it is safer to reveal more.

Finally, you may know the truth about why he cheated but refuse to accept it. It will still seem as if a piece of the puzzle is missing. In reality, you're just having a difficult time accepting the fact that he did indeed cheat. Cheating is inexcusable, you believe, so no reason for it could ever be good enough.

He May Feel Ashamed (Deep Down) for a Long Time

As I've stated, there are many good men (and women) who have affairs. When I speak to these men they struggle trying to accept themselves. They may have reasons for why they cheated but those reasons were not good enough in their hearts, either. You may think that it's appropriate he feels ashamed and you may even be thinking he deserves to suffer in any way possible. But my point is that in the years after an affair when a marriage has been restored, the infidelity can be a ugly part of his own past. It can always make him think less of himself. He has to somehow come to grips with what seems like a contradiction: "I'm a decent, honest man—who cheated on my wife and hurt my kids in the process." If his children were teenagers when the affair happened, they may have had strong negative opinions of their father. He may believe he lost his "hero" status with them. It is easy to focus completely on your own pain and victimization—and that is appropriate. But at some point it can be helpful to understand the price he may have paid, as well.

Ideas to Erase

Any idea that paralyzes you or makes you feel defeated before you've really begun must be tossed aside. The trouble is that your mind (your left brain) will insist that you think of every possible negative outcome and worst-case scenario to help you better prepare for that possibility. But unless you or your husband are seeking a divorce and have no intention whatsoever of salvaging the marriage, *it's too soon to tell* what will happen. Be realistic. If you both desire to reconcile you can succeed, although the process is difficult. For now, *accept* that you may be thinking very pessimistic thoughts and also accept that there are other ways to think.

You'll Never Be Able to Trust Him Again

Actually, trust can be restored. And if you wish to have any peace of mind it is important to trust. Always being skeptical and on edge cannot result in happiness. Day by day you will discover that he seems to be trustworthy and keeping his word. An unwillingness to trust is really your way of saying "I will not be made a fool of again." But you sacrifice happiness instead. Trust involves taking a risk. Anyone who reconciles with someone who has betrayed them must be willing to risk being betrayed again. Only you can decide if it is a risk worth taking. He will prove himself over time to be trustworthy or not.

You Should Have Seen the Signs

You may be driving yourself crazy by thinking back about all the signs you may have missed before your husband's affair was brought into the open. But if you are upset that you should have seen the signs and did not, you are focusing on the wrong issue. His affair is the issue, not how easily you put two and two together.

She Must Be Better than You

Making comparisons is normal and understandable. But if you make this a competition you take a lot of the anxiety away from your spouse—he should be worried about losing you more than you are worried about coming in second place to some other woman. If in the process of working things out you realize that you have made mistakes in the marriage, by all means aim to correct them. But that doesn't mean she is better than you. In fact, when a person leaves a marriage to be with an affair partner, that relationship succeeds only 10 percent of the time. Affair partners are not usually a better choice in the long run—they just appear to be in the short run. Also, when a man has an affair, the question is not what it is about "her" that makes her better than you. The question is this: How does he act when he's with her compared to when he's with you? Perhaps if he behaved with you the way he does with her, he might be happier with you.

Comparisons are a left-brain function. The left brain looks for details to determine what is better or worse. There is no peace of mind in the left brain, only stress and vigilance. You may have to accept that there are differences between you and the other woman—there are differences between you and everyone else on the planet. Those differences don't mean that she's better. She's . . . *different*. And differences can be appealing simply because they represent something new.

You Really Don't Know Him at All

It's possible that he led a completely double life—hidden bank accounts, many women on the side, friends you never knew existed, a past history totally different from what you were led to believe. But if his affair was typical of many, you know him better than you're admitting. On the negative side, perhaps he'd already shown himself to have addictive tendencies—gambling, alcohol, work, and so forth. Maybe you've heard him make up poor excuses for bad behavior. If so, his affair now represents more of the same and it probably isn't shocking. (If it is, you've been in denial about him.)

On the positive side, he may well be someone who in the past has shown himself to be someone with integrity, who was devoted to his family. Now he's cheated on you. Does that mean he never had integrity and never was devoted? If the marriage is to survive, you will have to be honest with yourself about the qualities of his character prior to the affair. If he acted in ways that you once respected and admired, chances are he still has those capabilities. True, his affair was a horrendous mistake. But black-and-white thinking will not serve you. If you believe he's a wonderful guy and ignore his affair, you're in denial. If you focus exclusively on his affair and view that as the hallmark of his character, you may also be in denial. He's more complicated than that, and so are most people.

If You Work Things Out You're Letting Him Off the Hook

What's the alternative? Holding him accountable the rest of his life? Will you be happy in a marriage like that? In some ways it's as if you were sitting patiently in your car at a red light, minding your own business, when *BOOM!* You were struck by another vehicle. Now you have a year of physical therapy, perhaps surgery, medications, and aches and pains, and it wasn't fair. You didn't deserve it. But you still must go through the work of healing because to not do so is to further harm yourself.

Imagine if you had a retaliatory affair. The score is even. Can you move forward in the marriage confidently now? Not likely. If you make the choice to remain in the marriage and to work to overcome the pain of infidelity, part of that work is letting go of justifiable anger and justifiable revenge. That means at some point you let him off the hook. Not because what he did wasn't so bad, but because it's bad for you to allow what he did to forever scar your marriage and your heart.

The Victim and the Persecutor

Enraged by the affair and frightened about what it means for your future, your mind will spin beliefs and ideas that make you sometimes act like a persecutor and sometimes like a victim.

Persecuting accusations include:

- "You're despicable and a liar."
- "Once a cheater always a cheater."
- "You don't care about your kids!"

Victimization beliefs include:

- "I can never be happy again."
- "What did I ever do to deserve this?"
- "I always tried my best to be a good wife. How could he do this to me?"

Both sets of beliefs are common and both become destructive to you and the marriage over time. You may find yourself in a typical circular pattern of misery:

1. You persecute your husband for his treachery.
2. Exhausted and anguished from persecuting, you focus on how you've been victimized.
3. Frightened that the marriage is doomed, you put aside your victim mentality somewhat and try to save your marriage.
4. Your efforts to salvage the marriage or give your husband some degree of understanding eventually just make you madder. You hate that this whole thing ever happened and resent that you must suffer not only from his cheating but from the pain of trying to reconcile or to figure out where the rest of your life is headed.

5. Furious, you now persecute him again.
6. A persecuting stance leads to feeling victimized, which leads to efforts to make repairs, which leads to more persecution, and the cycle keeps repeating.

Exhausting and draining, isn't it?

It's easy for me to tell you to simply stop that pattern, but in the weeks and months following an affair that can be difficult to achieve. However, perhaps by recognizing the pattern you can see that you are not gaining any ground and are just spinning your wheels. All that emotional energy is being wasted—and you're depleted enough as it is. When you feel you've had enough of the merry-go-round, you will have to *accept* that the affair happened and not resist it (taking a persecutory or victimization stance is in opposition to the real work that needs to be done). Once you've accepted it, you will continue to feel sad. Sadness is a clean emotion. It reflects an honest awareness of loss. Then, more productive work can occur.

getting a grip 2: the next most important things to do

It's been a chaotic, gut-wrenching time for you. And depending upon how long it has been since the affair was discovered, your thoughts, feelings, and actions may be completely out of whack with one another. Your head says one thing one minute, your heart says something else (and something else again), and your actions would make anybody who was watching dizzy. In a brief span of one hour you might vent rage, be overwhelmed with fear, jerk away from any closeness with him, push for togetherness, demand answers from him, refuse to accept any answers as anything but lies or excuses, want him in your life, want him out of your life, threaten him, plead with him, blame yourself, blame him—and this happens every day for days on end.

You don't know how you feel or what you think or what you want because you're still trying to process what happened and deal with new information as it arrives. You're obsessed and you're exhausted from obsessing. But somehow you must function. You must get up in the morning, go to work, and take care of your kids while your future seems to hang in the balance.

Setting Up Rules for Your Guy

At this point in time, you actually have two different jobs you must perform in order to get a grip and move on with your life. You have to take steps to deal with the organization of your life—including what temporary guidelines to set up regarding your husband—and you must manage the inner turmoil in yourself.

If your husband expresses at least some desire to see if the marriage can work out you will need to set up some strict guidelines (temporarily) to help keep your anxiety lower and to gain confidence that he is making a serious effort.

Step 1: Focus on Rebuilding or at Least Not Ending the Marriage

Before one or both of you makes a decision about the fate of your marriage, it is best to set a somewhat arbitrary time frame in which both of you focus on the possibility of rebuilding the marriage, rather than ending it.

It is unwise to demand that he fully commit to you 100 percent or that he be absolutely certain he wants to be with you for the rest of his life. He may very well have mixed feelings (as may you). Forcing him to declare something he knows he cannot declare may destroy chances of healing the marriage before efforts begin. However, despite his ambivalence, it's quite possible for him to commit to working on the relationship to see if it can be salvaged. If he is uncertain about staying with you, he may only agree to hang in there for a short period of time (say, a month or two). Ideally, give yourselves a period of three to six months in which you will each try to see if the marriage can work and during which you will not give up. At the end of that predetermined time frame, you can each reassess your situation. Has there been progress? Is it worth committing to more time?

Step 2: Set Up Rules and Restrictions for Him

When you decide upon restrictions regarding where he can go and what he can do, your husband will absolutely feel like a punished child or a prisoner. The purpose is not to humiliate him or punish him. The purpose is to make it easier for you to begin to trust him. As trust grows, restrictions can be removed. Common restrictions may include:

- He cannot hang out with friends after work.
- He must not be casual about what time he arrives home from work. If he is going to be late he must call and have a valid reason.
- His cell phone and e-mails must be accessible to you.
- You have the right if you so choose to go through his things— look in his wallet and check the inside of his car, his dresser drawers, his coat pockets, and so on.
- He must report any contact he has with the other woman, even if it was a chance meeting or passing by her in a car or in a hallway at work. If she initiates contact just to say "Hi" he must report that.
- He must be receptive and cooperative when you ask questions such as "Where were you this afternoon? Did you go anywhere else? Did you make any phone calls while you were out? Did you see anyone you knew while you were out? Where are you going now? How long will you be?"

Those are not the only restrictions possible. You might have several more unique to your situation. If he balks at these restrictions or grows impatient with them, try to keep your cool. Your best response: "I'm not controlling you or forcing you to do anything. You can choose to do what you want. However, if you choose to not go along with these temporary restrictions I will have a much harder time trusting you and our relationship will continue to be rocky." If he says you are threatening him, respond this way: "I'm telling you that there are consequences to the choices you made. If you choose to cooperate with me, I have a better chance of believing in you. If you won't, I am likely to conclude that you have something to hide and that I cannot trust you."

Step 3: Be Cautious about Compulsive Gathering of Evidence

If the affair was recent, or if you have reason to believe your spouse might still be lying to you and carrying on with the other woman, looking for evidence may be your next step. In extreme examples, people do such things as secretly tape phone conversations; install computer software that gives them access to another person's online activities; use tracking devices on cars; use friends to set their partner up in a situation (at a bar, online) and see if he takes the bait; or hire a private investigator.

Many women have told me, "I searched through his glove compartment (or dresser drawers, or computer files) and found letters from his mistress. I know it was wrong of me to do that . . ." I beg to differ. If he cheated on you and lied and perhaps has still been lying, he is putting your future and your emotional life (and your children's) at stake. You have every reason to search for evidence. However, there is a limit to how much evidence-gathering you should do. Done too frequently it can become addictive and destructive to your purpose.

Data collection can never prove his innocence or that he is telling the truth. It can only prove guilt. Women who become obsessed with data collection follow a pattern. First they have anxiety about his trustworthiness or about being made a fool of. They search for data. If they find evidence, that reinforces the need to look again. If they find no evidence, it can alleviate their anxiety temporarily—and that is a highly rewarding feeling. People can become addicted to easing their anxiety by seeking out evidence, rather than easing their anxiety in some other, more adaptive way. If done compulsively, data gathering will leave you feeling like a drug addict. You'll feel temporarily satisfied and need another fix later on. There is no rule about when to halt data gathering. But the longer it goes on, the more it will complicate your situation. As soon as you think you can limit data gathering, do so. Cut back and perhaps on occasion do a random search. But eventually all such data gathering must cease if you want to be happy in the relationship.

Step 4: Speak with an Attorney

You need to know your rights and you need to know what to expect if a legal separation or divorce ensues. This can be a one-shot consultation. Sometimes a spouse will threaten to take the kids or leave you impoverished if you seek a divorce. Knowing what a realistic legal outcome is can ease your mind. Or you may learn that your post-separation status will not be very good. Maybe it will mean relocating, having to take on a second job, or living with your parents. It's best to know these things ahead of time rather than make any impulsive decisions and be unprepared for the consequences.

Step 5: Find Time for Civility

Too much negativity is not helpful. You may not feel warm toward your mate but it's still advisable to be civil whenever possible and seek moments of pleasantness or even thoughtfulness. These can be low-key moments—asking if he needs something at the store while you're out, or inquiring about his day at work or how his mother is feeling these days.

What If Your Best Girlfriend Had an Affair?

If your best friend had an affair would you reject her even if you disapproved? If your friend's husband was so angry he wanted a divorce and your friend was repentant and remorseful, would you see any value in the two of them trying to work it out? Might you say, "I don't approve of what you did but given the circumstances I can understand why it may have happened"? If so, perhaps you can find it within yourself to see the value of healing your relationship even though you're justified in being furious and rejecting.

You're entitled to be angry, standoffish, petty, and cold, but it's not in your best interest to be that way most of the time. Softening the edges of your relationship here or there can soothe your emotions and offer hope that the relationship can heal. If he wants to reconcile and you are mostly hostile, rejecting, aloof, unfriendly, and controlling—that's understandable. But what if he had the affair in part because he was feeling lonely, rejected, ignored, and unappreciated? You'd be offering him more of the very thing that whittled away his commitment to you. Think of something about him that you have loved or admired in the past or think of something you have sympathy for and use that as the motivation to offer him small doses of kindness.

Step 6: Be Aware of "Accusatory Suffering"

Author and family therapist Gerald Weeks uses this term to describe the act of holding on to one's suffering for fear that if you begin to let go of it the perpetrator will minimize his actions. If your husband is a narcissist and unable to show genuine remorse, holding on to your pain as a way to get him to see how he damaged you won't work. And if he is remorseful for his actions, holding on to your pain for longer than is needed will have an opposite effect. Many guilt-ridden men will shy away from their wives when the women are suffering precisely because it is a painful reminder to the men of how much harm they've caused.

To avoid accusatory suffering doesn't mean you can't show pain. That would be faking it. But it means that as time goes by you will serve your deepest needs better by being less intense about how you reveal your pain. Throwing it in his face, giving him the cold shoulder, or being emotionally flat happens a lot in the roller-coaster and subdued phases (see Chapter 1) of coping with infidelity. But ideally those reactions ease up over time. Your husband is more likely to be sympathetic to your pain over the long haul if you can "report" your feelings ("I'm just having a bad day. I've been thinking a lot about your affair recently even though we've made progress. Bear with me.") rather than demonstrate them aggressively. When he doesn't have to defend himself, talk you out of your misery, or avoid you for fear of what you will say or do, he is more likely to approach you with sensitivity and caring.

Managing What's Going on Inside You

You've actually already started. Gaining perspective from reading the previous chapters, learning which thoughts to embrace and which to erase, and learning to be more emotionally accepting of the situation while you take steps to deal with it all help you to manage your inner life.

Now you need to go deeper. At the first level of personal inquiry in any emotional upheaval, you examine the facts of what happened, take stock of how you're feeling, and figure out what steps to begin taking. For example, if your car was banged up you'd have to make decisions about repairs, getting a rental, or maybe purchasing a new vehicle. You might feel angry or worried and would try to manage your emotions. You are making first-level inquiries now as you initially deal with infidelity and will continue to make more inquiries as your personal situation unfolds. The first level is more immediately reactive and more practical. But it's time to begin a second, deeper level of inquiry. Everyone has sore spots. All of us, by virtue of our early experiences in life, develop a set of beliefs about ourselves—accurate or distorted—and we carry that theme with us as we move through life. If the theme is positive and growth enhancing ("I can handle what life dishes out and turn tough times into good times") you are at an advantage. If the theme is negative and blunts growth ("I'm not lovable; I don't deserve to be happy") you will be at a disadvantage when trying to cope with adversity.

Think about your childhood. Think about how your parents got along, whether or not home life was stable and warm or unstable and hostile. Did you have to put up with things you didn't like? Did you have to grow up fast and oversee younger siblings? Did you have to fend for yourself emotionally as you got older because one or both of your parents was not approachable to talk to? Were you victimized? Rejected? Did you have a lot of power? No power? Did you have to be perfect? Did you put aside your needs for the sake of others? Were you mistreated? Misunderstood? Bullied?

As you think about those questions there is one final question it's important to answer. (This is taken from Harville Hendrix's popular book *Getting the Love You Want.*) The question is this: What did you want from your childhood but not get (or not get enough of)?

The odds are very good that you still struggle with that theme now as an adult. In the aftermath of your husband's infidelity, that underlying theme might get triggered and interfere with your coping.

For example, Jan was raised by alcoholic parents and had to look after her siblings since she was the oldest. If something went wrong—as it often did—she blamed herself. She felt she should somehow prevent family problems from happening. So when her husband admitted to a brief affair, she immediately blamed herself.

Jill was a happy child until her parents split up. Her father rarely visited the children and she felt abandoned. She developed an embedded belief that "I'm not important or worthwhile." So when her husband was caught having an online relationship with a woman it triggered those old beliefs.

Think of a childhood or young-adult memory that still hurts. What negative belief about you does that trigger? Some possibilities might include:

- I'm not lovable.
- I'm inadequate.
- I'm helpless or powerless.
- It's all my fault.
- I don't deserve happiness.
- I can't trust.
- I'm shameful.
- My body is ugly.

The themes you come up with will fall into one or more of four broad categories: loss of lovability; loss of self-esteem; loss of control or influence; loss of safety or security. That's important to understand because when you locate where you feel most vulnerable it points you in a direction. If your husband's cheating affected your self-esteem most of all ("I'm not desirable") then winning back your husband (or not) isn't the whole answer for you. Other steps must be taken down the road to enhance your esteem, whether that means changing your diet and exercise regimen, going back to school, finding new hobbies that will make you feel accomplished, or learning to wholeheartedly accept yourself and your good qualities. If your sense of control over your life was in tatters after his affair, controlling his actions won't work in the long run. Instead you may need to learn how to "go with the flow" since controlling all outcomes is not possible. What could you do over the next twelve months that would make you feel more lovable? More safe and secure? Start a list and begin making headway on it now. It will distract you from the issue of his affair (you need a distraction) while allowing you to improve your ability to cope.

Overcoming Knee-Jerk Responses

The kind of responses you've had since learning of the infidelity—whether they are intellectual, emotional, or behavioral responses—have probably been highly reactive (almost *nuclear* reactive). Heightened reactivity is perfectly normal and yet usually works against you. Reactivity has nothing to do with volume. You can be as quiet as a mouse but be intensely emotional on the inside. Your reactivity—how you instantly think, feel, or act when faced with a crisis—represents a long-standing trait. A quick reaction is good in a crisis because often you have little time to think (such as when you suddenly slam on the brakes to avoid a collision). Thinking slows you down. Knee-jerk reactions give you an edge. But knee-jerk reactions are best in a short-term crisis, not for coping over the long haul. Your goal now is to be smart, not reckless. The harm done by reckless comments and actions in the aftermath of an affair can obstruct healing. You've probably said and done many reckless, knee-jerk things since learning of your husband's infidelity. You may have called him names, shut him out, kicked him out, threatened him, hit him, begged him—and none of it really helped. Automatic, knee-jerk actions often leave you second-guessing yourself later, or petrified that you may have crossed a line, made a fool of yourself, or hurt your chances of healing the relationship. And if those highly reactive responses continue, he'll become gun-shy. He'll be afraid to talk to you, to answer questions, or to reach out when you want him to reach out precisely because he fears a flash-fire response.

Knee-jerk, intense reactions make perfect sense after an affair. They're not wrong and there is no absolute rule saying not to react immediately. However, you will serve your needs better when you can be less reactive to the moment and more responsive to your higher goals.

People in your shoes may have different kinds of knee-jerk responses. Your personality can play a role (hyper, more passionate people may react with outward intensity while quieter, reserved people may react with a great deal of inner turmoil that isn't always displayed). Your life circumstances can affect your response. If you'd fallen out of love with your husband and he had an affair, you might not care much. But if you're young, in love, and expecting a baby, his affair can be devastating. If his affair triggered some past hurt (say, your father cheated on your mother and things were never the same for you after that) you may feel more vulnerable than if you were raised in a stable, loving, encouraging home. It's useful to contemplate this idea: *You are suffering now for more reasons than you think.* If you limit your understanding of why you are reacting so hotly and suffering so much pain to the obvious reason—he cheated on you—you will be frustrated when the marriage seems to improve yet your pain seems to never really subside. Or you will be disheartened when you seem unable to improve your relationship and your suffering continues on and on.

You are not troubled for only the reasons you think. And furthermore, he may not have cheated for the reasons he thinks. Both of you are probably operating from your unconscious, to some extent. The more you can make your unconscious become conscious, the better shot you have at managing your emotions and healing the wound of betrayal.

Making Your Unconscious Mind Conscious

This is no straightforward task. It is a lifetime process but you can make strides that will help you now. Review Chapter 4 on emotional acceptance. If you can come to accept each thought you have and each moment you are in instead of being emotionally opposed to them ("This shouldn't be happening!"), you will have better access to your unconscious mind. Resisting the moment blocks access to your unconscious. Imagine that you have ten layers of thoughts, ten layers to the onion of your mind, in response to the betrayal. Imagine that the first four layers are conscious thoughts (there could be dozens of them), the next four layers are subconscious but close to the surface, and the final two layers are well beneath your awareness.

Your first layer might include the thought "Our marriage may not survive." A subconscious layer might include the thought "Nobody will want me." An unconscious thought might be "I don't deserve happiness and am helpless to do anything." If you spend most of your energy trying to control your husband, arguing with him, or collapsing in your room and worrying, you may only have access to your conscious thoughts and never deal with the underlying beliefs. If your deepest belief is "I'm helpless" then you may sabotage your own efforts to make the relationship work or give up too quickly because you are being controlled by an unconscious belief that says you cannot succeed by your efforts.

That's why examining your inner life is crucial. It also buys you time. You don't need to make all the key decisions now. You don't need to figure out your future right now (and you probably can't—there are still too many unknowns at the moment). If you stop fighting with your spouse and with yourself and simply accept each passing thought and feeling (because it is your reality of the moment), your inner thoughts can chug along into your awareness without having to pause while you spend precious time arguing with reality.

Fill in the incomplete sentences below. Try to come up with seven to ten (or even more) responses for each statement. The answers that come quickly are the most conscious. Keep trying after you can't think of any more "obvious" answers. If you allow yourself to meditate for several minutes on each question, you may come up with answers that will surprise you and be more helpful to you as you cope with the infidelity.

1. I will feel more at peace when

_____

_____.

2. This hurt reminds me of

_____

_____.

3. My greatest strength is

_____

_____.

4. If I were my husband I would most be in need of

_____

_____.

5. The absolute worst thing that could happen now is

_____

_____.

6. I am capable of giving love even when

_____

_____.

7. My soul (highest self) wants me to

_____

_____.

8. The silver lining behind this cloud is

_____

_____.

9. When I look back upon this time ten years from now I will

_____

_____.

Regrouping

The first six chapters offer a balance between actions you need to take in your outer environment and things you need to do manage your inner self. Doing one without the other will result in setbacks and perhaps failure. The tendency for many people in your situation is to confuse obsessive rumination and worry with "working on my inner self." Worry, especially worry that leads in no useful direction, is the opposite of patiently examining your thoughts, feelings, embedded beliefs, and subconscious motivations. Obsessive worry is akin to spinning your tires but going nowhere. Since your situation is evolving, you will continue to learn more about yourself and your deeper motivations as you move on with your life—with or without your spouse. So feel free to return to this chapter periodically.

Now it's time to learn how to talk about the affair with your spouse in the way that is the most effective and will increase the chances that you can heal and move forward.

talking it out: lifesaving strategies

You've probably stumbled your way through many rocky conversations about his cheating by now. Most couples don't have perfectly honed communication skills even under calm circumstances. After an infidelity, when emotions skyrocket and doubts multiply, whatever skills a couple does possess fly out the door. But you must somehow talk about what happened, why it happened, and where the two of you will go from here.

Good communication skills aren't really about following strict, polite rules such as "take turns," "don't interrupt," and "don't mind-read." In fact, the happiest of couples often break the commonsense conversation rules and suffer no ill-effects. Why? Because they possess a large storehouse of goodwill and are able to manage their emotions more effectively while conversing. Any formula for effective communication that works does so because it helps you keep your emotions from taking control. When emotions run amuck you will either fly off the handle or shut down—and either response will complicate, perhaps cripple, your conversation. Later in this chapter you will learn about the SAIL technique I created to help couples stay on course in very rough conversational seas. But there are several things you need to know first.

Talking about Cheating

If you are watching a gripping movie or stage play, you may be unaware that what makes the story enthralling is not just the action sequences or the dialogue but the subtext. The subtext has to do with what *isn't* being said but is nevertheless driving the scene forward. For example, imagine two young lovers gazing in each other's eyes as the young man is about to go off to war, perhaps never to return.

She finally says to him "Goodbye." One word—but it's packed with emotion and says so much.

When you and your partner start to discuss his cheating, you'll be swimming in subtext. Each of you will be looking for hidden meanings. Offhand comments such as "I'm fine" will really mean just the opposite. If he wants to end the discussion you'll view him as not caring or as having something to hide. It's best to point out the subtext when you become aware of it. For example:

You ask questions and he responds with one-word answers. The subtext from your perspective is that you think he isn't being cooperative. (From his perspective, maybe he'd rather not talk at that time.) Rather than just getting frustrated you say, "You keep giving me one-word answers. I'm not sure if that means you don't want to talk or if you're afraid of something. Can you make your answers more informative?" Or he might say, "I guess I'm not that responsive because now isn't a good time to talk. Can we do this later today?"

When he is with you, you give him the cold shoulder but you also wish moments together could be less intense. Instead of allowing those contradictory emotions to dominate the moment you say, "I have mixed emotions when I'm with you. I want us to find some time to be more at ease but I'm also extremely hurt and angry. Try to understand."

He acts aloof around you. You say, "I notice you keep to yourself more. I don't know if you don't want me around, if you have thinking to do, or if you don't know how to act around me. Any thoughts?"

The idea is to put on the table in a clear way what would otherwise be ambiguous or confusing and open to wrong interpretations. Imagine in the last example that he is acting aloof around you but you do not address that straightforwardly. You will then do one of two things. You will make your own interpretations (perhaps mistaken) and act on those interpretations by withdrawing or by being argumentative. If your interpretation was wrong, your behavior will now seem strange or out of line to him. Or you will make an interpretation and present it as an accusation rather than as a possibility. "You act so cold around me! Obviously you're thinking of her and wish I wasn't around!" If he denies it, you may not believe him. Regardless, he will get frustrated and be even less likely to interact with you for fear of more unfair confrontations.

Do You Both Agree about Your Future?

It's common after an infidelity for one or both of you to be unsure whether you want the marriage to proceed. You and he could go on for months without clarity. *As time passes without a clear decision to work on the marriage, the decision is really being made to move on from the marriage.* That may not be the intent, but it's the practical fallout from a failure to commit to seeing if the marriage is salvageable. Similarly, the longer he remains torn between feelings for you and feelings for her, the worse it is for the marriage. Your marriage cannot remain on hold for any extended period of time while he (or you) remains indecisive. A long period of indecision results in more arguments, more disdain, more heartbreak, more rage, heightened anxiety for every family member—all of which pulls him closer to the other woman, who is a greater source of comfort. (It's possible the other woman won't wait for him to decide, either. But she can probably afford to be more patient.)

Trying to discuss the affair and have productive conversations with your husband will be frustrating if one or both of you isn't even sure you want the marriage to continue. *But you don't have to decide now if you want to remain together forever. You do need to decide if you will give the relationship a fair shot by working on it in a committed way for at least the next few months.* After that you can reassess the situation and decide if it is worth continuing the process.

If your husband is totally confused about who he wants to be with, no amount of arguing or crying will help him choose you. In fact, if he feels pressure from you he may conclude that if he returned to you it would be because he felt forced—not because he wanted to of his own free will. Your options now are limited. You could separate temporarily (but he might spend his time with the other woman). You could make the decision for both of you and proceed with a divorce. Perhaps the best option for now is to let him know that you are open to seeing if reconciliation is possible but that as time goes on you may become less open. That must not be a threat but a true statement of how you feel. You might say something like this:

"It's clear to me that you cannot decide. I want to see if our marriage can work and I'm not ready to give up. But I can't force you. In the next few weeks I will speak to an attorney so I know what to expect if we end up separated or divorced. In the meantime I will be civil toward you and open to discussions. If as the weeks go by you still cannot decide to work on our relationship I know I will become less hopeful and more resigned to the fact that we might end up divorced. At some point I won't want to work out our problems even if you change your mind."

You may feel some of those words don't fit your personality or that you couldn't say them sincerely. But those words serve a clear purpose. Let's presume that your husband cannot make up his mind if he wants you or her and he feels pulled equally in both directions. If you try to plead with him or threaten him as a way to pull him toward you, he will resist and be drawn toward her. However, if you pull away from him somewhat—not in anger or as a manipulation but as an honest act of personal integrity—he will be in touch with the idea of losing you and therefore be more drawn toward you.

If during the following weeks you suspect he is seeing her a lot, you may need to decide to seek a separation sooner. He is allowed to have mixed feelings. He is allowed to miss her even if he is staying with you. But if he is involved with her in any way, the odds that he will be able to commit to you and the marriage are against you.

Man-Talk Versus Woman-Talk

If you and your husband agree to see if your marriage can work after his affair, many conversational pitfalls await you. You are seeking the truth about what happened and a way to determine if your marriage will succeed or fail. But the manner in which those conversations occur may make or break your relationship. Your primary subtext now is that you don't trust him. That colors everything. His subtext (assuming he wants to make the marriage work) is that you will never forgive him and the two of you will never be happy again. So during conversations you will be sniffing out evidence of whether he is being honest, and he will be searching for any hint that you and he can one day put this in the past.

Research findings indicate that when there is an area of conflict, women will start those conversations harshly. Harsh startups predict that the conversation will end in failure. It will cause the man to escalate in kind and to quickly shut down. Shutting down from conversations predicts relationship unhappiness. And each reaction tends to provoke the other. The more harsh the conversation, the more likely someone will end it abruptly. When a conversation shuts down before it's completed, the likelihood increases that the next conversation will begin harshly.

In the days following the exposure of an affair, it's almost impossible to have constructive, noninflammatory conversations. But over time it becomes essential that one's emotional reactions be measured. The previous chapters actually help you in that regard. As you come to understand why he may have cheated, you will be able to recognize irrational embedded beliefs you have that only make matters worse, and as you understand what the deeper layers of hurt for you might be, you stand a better chance of having conversations that combine smarts with sensitivity—not irrationality with hysteria.

Scheduling Conversations

You need to know information. He needs to provide it. And you both need times when you can count on *not* having a difficult conversation so that opportunities for quieter (or even more pleasant) interactions can happen. If you are like the typical betrayed spouse you will find yourself starting heavy discussions at random moments, whenever the mood strikes. He will often balk at that, especially if you awaken him at two in the morning to talk or if the discussions drag on for hours. You will regard his balking as a sign of his insensitivity to your feelings and perhaps as his way to still keep secrets. He will regard your insistence on talking at any time as equivalent to a drive-by shooting. The upshot will be that he will become less and less cooperative and you will be more and more demanding.

A useful strategy is to schedule discussions at prearranged times. Discussion should not last longer than one hour. The frequency of the discussions can be up to you, depending upon how obsessed and preoccupied you are. I suggest that in the beginning you limit discussions to three times a week or less and as time goes on make them less frequent. A scheduled discussion allows you the opportunity you need to vent and to ask questions—even if you asked the same questions a hundred times already. And it allows him the opportunity to be less on edge, knowing that he can relax during dinner or watching a movie and that you will not spontaneously demand answers to more questions.

There are three rules that must be followed to make this effective:

1. Do not talk longer than the allotted time unless you are both in complete agreement. If he says he does not wish to talk after an hour, so be it.
2. He must be receptive to all questions and cooperate in the process. He is not to complain that you're asking a question yet again or challenge you in any way. He shouldn't roll his eyes or give any nonverbal signal that he is bored, annoyed, or fed up by your questions or this process.

3. Do not punish him or be cold to each other after the conversation. You may or may not feel like being in each other's presence but don't come off as punitive. Better to thank each other for following the rules and attempt to at least be civil toward each other.

If there were unresolved marital problems prior to the affair, your husband may prefer to discuss those rather than always focusing on his infidelity. You can also schedule discussions in which those broader marital concerns will be the focus. Especially when you get to the rebuilding phase, your discussions will not be limited to the affair.

How to De-Escalate

It's not essential that you avoid intense emotional moments during conversations. They're bound to happen, especially when the stakes are high. The problem is not a high level of intensity but rather a level of intensity that continues to rise with no de-escalation. If one or both of you becomes more and more intense as you speak, or if the intensity between you escalates so that you each respond to the other with increasing force (much like a verbal tennis match where you each hit the ball back at ever increasing speeds), the conversation will probably fail. Failed conversations set up a self-fulfilling prophecy so future conversations will be high in anxiety and likely to fail as well.

To de-escalate it helps to put aside your role of persecutor or victim before you go into the conversation. You have been victimized and you may feel like persecuting him, which will in turn make him feel like a victim. But those stances will impede your ultimate goal.

The simplest way to de-escalate is to either acknowledge that something your spouse is saying has merit or admit that you are saying things in a way you shouldn't be.

For example:

- "I shouldn't have said that. Let me try again."
- "I was wrong just now to call you a liar."
- "I agree with you when you say . . ."

Or you could point out when he is escalating but do so in way that is nonconfrontational:

- "You're raising your voice now. I want to understand you but I need you to speak more calmly."
- "When you say such things I'd ordinarily argue back and we'd just escalate. Let's not do that. Can you rephrase what you just said?"
- "We're both just throwing daggers. Can we agree to stop the name-calling and try to talk more civilly?"

Be careful. If you add the word "but" to those comments, as in "I agree with what you say *but* . . ." you're headed for another escalation. Too often one spouse will try to de-escalate while the other keeps ramping up the voltage. It's a good idea before you begin the conversation to agree that if one of you tries to de-escalate, the other will cooperate.

Should You Shut Down a Too-Intense Conversation?

It's often the case that one person—usually the man—will ask to take a break or postpone the rest of the conversation when it's too intense. If the woman is unwilling, she may even follow him around the house as he tries to escape. If in fact one person is overwhelmed it's a good idea to take a break. But the goal must be to return to the conversation within half an hour. During the break it's important that each of you not focus on what's wrong with your spouse but instead on how you can make the conversation go more smoothly.

The SAIL Approach to Communication

If conversations were like roads, the SAIL approach would be a direct route to get where you're going. Most intense conversations get off track fast and cover too much territory. Certainly your situation now isn't a simple one to talk about, let alone resolve. There are many issues you must face. But whenever your talks start to get out of control, the SAIL approach will put you back on track. The good news is that if you've taken to heart the previous chapters you've already begun learning SAIL. It includes four major steps that begin with the letters S, A, I, and L:

1. **State straightforwardly** your point without judgment, harshness, or detours into unproductive areas. Don't attack; keep it simple.

2. **Accept** what your partner thinks, feels, says, and does during the conversation instead of being emotionally opposed to it. You don't have to like it, agree with it, or go along with it. But don't insist he shouldn't be responding the way he is.

3. **Inquire** more deeply into the issue at hand. Why is it so important? What personal experiences does it remind you of? What issues lie beneath the obvious ones? What's at stake for you?

4. **List** creative ideas to make headway on resolving the concerns.

When couples are discussing thorny issues and come away with some kind of positive reaction to their conversation, it's because they have used all four elements of SAIL. Those elements allow partners to feel listened to, understood, respected, and accepted—and to come away with a plan. While I encourage you to apply this approach as soon as possible, betrayed spouses find it hard to do so in the roller coaster phase of recovery when emotions are at their most intense. But as soon as you apply this approach, your discussions will be more effective. Let's examine each one more closely.

State Your Thoughts Straightforwardly

Perhaps your spouse can handle it if you scream or cry or call him names. Maybe he feels he has it coming. But over time he will grow weary and fear the relationship will never heal. Anyone who is being attacked soon becomes defensive. It's a natural response. A defensive person doesn't listen well. He doesn't try to understand the spirit of your message. He'll either bear it and wait until the storm has passed, give up on the conversation, or become angry and accusatory himself. Emotional upheaval during conversations about betrayal and infidelity is common. But the sooner you can manage your emotions the better. You must be mindful when your words are cutting and your tone is harsh. Keep it simple. Describe his actions (or what you suspect might have been his actions) and state what that makes you think and what feelings follow from your thoughts. You need not go precisely in that order. For example, imagine he is late arriving home from work and you worried that he might have been meeting up with *her*. He denies it. So later in your scheduled conversation you might say: "When you arrived home late I couldn't help but worry about what you were doing. And when I asked you about it you got annoyed that I don't trust you. It makes me angry that I'm made to appear overly suspicious when I'm trying to recover from your affair. I need you to be more sensitive to that." In those four sentences you described his actions and your thoughts and feelings about his actions, and made a request for change.

Pay attention to your nonverbal behavior. Loud sighs, head shaking, eye-rolling, or finger-pointing can be just as inflammatory as a harsh putdown. There are two other ways to keep the conversation from escalating:

- Remain seated during the discussion. Talks while standing up have a greater tendency to escalate.
- Try to speak in a tone of voice similar to normal, everyday conversation—or even more subdued. Research shows that the act of speaking more loudly while upset actually makes you feel even more upset; and speaking more quietly when upset can make you feel less upset.

Accept What's Happening in the Moment

This is a crucial concept and was discussed at length in Chapter 4. To be emotionally accepting doesn't mean you must be passive or allow a spouse to do things you don't like. It means not getting agitated about it in the process. Imagine you ask him a question about his relationship with the other woman and he gets annoyed because you've asked that same question before. "Are you bringing that up *again?*" he says with irritation. You have every reason to be angry at his attitude. After all, he cheated on you. You wouldn't be asking him those questions if he hadn't broken a marriage vow. If you rail at him he might realize his mistake and do better next time. But he might just be more resentful. And if his feelings about you are already mixed, you may be pushing him away.

So say to yourself, "I accept that he has the wrong attitude about my need to ask questions." Then let him know that you will probably be asking many questions over again and you'd appreciate it if he'd cooperate. Don't get into a "How dare you have that attitude!" moment. That's not acceptance. Notice in this example that *he was not accepting* of the fact that you asked him a question he'd already answered before. His lack of acceptance added to the tension in the moment. If he were emotionally accepting, he still might wish you wouldn't repeat questions but he'd state that differently. He might say, "I know you still don't trust me or believe everything I say. But when I have to answer the same question over and over I feel we may never get past this." By being accepting of you, he still can get his point across and you will have an easier time listening.

You know you're not emotionally accepting your spouse's comments when you respond with statements like "How can you say that? . . .

I can't believe you just said that! . . . How dare you say such a thing!" If you find what he said to be offensive or insensitive, ask him to start again and rephrase it. Tell him you didn't like it. But don't fight him on the fact that he said it.

Emotional acceptance is the precursor to understanding. You will stop trying to understand what you already refuse to accept.

Acceptance is important in difficult conversations because neither you nor your spouse is a perfect communicator or operating from your highest level of competence or emotional maturity right now. You're both exhausted, scared, and under the gun. Cut each other some slack.

Inquire about the Deeper Meaning

Many of your early talks will be about data gathering. When did he see her? How often? Where did they go? What did they do? How often did they talk on the phone? Once you have that information, you'll ask him things like "Did you talk to her today? Did you think of her today? Do you miss her?" Those conversations are usually necessary, although arduous, painful, and gut-wrenching. But you can create more closeness when you each go deeper. He needs to try to understand why he did what he did and why the other woman seemed so important to him that he risked his marriage and family life for her. And you need to examine what underlying issues his infidelity is touching on for you.

When David cheated on his wife Anne, he said that Anne spent too much time on their children and ignored him. It had been a long-standing, divisive issue. When he met Sandy, she of course lavished attention on him. He felt desired, cared about, and important. At home with Anne he felt more like a paycheck and "the hired help." Anne was furious that he cheated on her and told him he was immature to expect her to give him all the attention he wanted while they had children to raise. She regarded his reason for the affair as a self-serving excuse made by a man who needs to "grow up."

By using the SAIL approach they began to talk to each other without harshness or judging. Anne "accepted" his reasons for the affair by being willing to understand them more—not attack him for feeling the way he did. She didn't like hearing his reasons but she accepted that was how he felt. As David looked deeper into his psyche, he spoke about his childhood. Dad was away a lot, Mom had her hands full with five kids and since he was the oldest he put aside many of his own needs to help out more around the house. So now when Anne was paying a lot less attention to him because of the children, it tapped into that old feeling David had of never getting to have his needs met. *That does not excuse his cheating.* But it makes it a bit more understandable. For her part, Anne had a lot of insecurities growing up. Never very popular and not as attractive as many of the other girls, she shied away from dating. Once she and David had children she realized that her role as a devoted mom was something she felt really good about. So, perhaps unwittingly, she pulled away from David somewhat and always justified it by saying that the kids came first. Eventually, David felt left out.

By understanding these deeper issues it gave them room to maneuver without taking each other's actions so personally. David understood why it was important for Anne to be a very involved mother, and Anne really understood that David was feeling neglected.

List Ways to Address the Problem

Couples who struggle with communication often do so because they never get to the part of the conversation that goes "What are we willing to do about this?" Instead they debate "facts" and try to use coercion or verbal persuasion to get the other person to see things one way. For example, let's go back to David and Anne. Once they got to the "L" in SAIL they first reverted to the old debate. She said he shouldn't have had an affair. Period. He said she was overinvolved with and too protective of the kids. He said he was sorry she felt so insecure as a child but that was no excuse to pay so little attention to him now. She said she was sorry he had so many responsibilities as a child and couldn't get his needs met but now they were parents and parents must learn to put the children's needs ahead of their own. So I asked them: "Given your understanding of what the other wants and needs, what are each of you *willing to do* that will address at least some of your partner's needs?" Eventually, David agreed to spend more time taking care of the kids so Anne had free time for other things. And she agreed to hire a sitter more often and spend some of her free time paying attention to him. Anne realized that it was hard for her to let David be in charge of the children because childrearing was her primary way of feeling good about herself and that perhaps she had been overinvolved with them. And David realized that once he felt neglected by Anne he'd spent less time at home, which made him feel needier of her time when he was home. So in addition to the proposed changes, Anne realized she needed a fascinating hobby that would add to her sense of accomplishment. She chose to volunteer at a local community theater and get involved in stage productions. And Dave agreed to be supportive of that and use her time away as an opportunity to be more "hands on" with their children.

Any list you come up with is not a permanent solution. Relationships and personal needs always fluctuate. So you'll have to revisit the "What are we willing to do?" question many times. But without getting to that step, you will never come up with answers you can both live with.

In the aftermath of an affair you may also have an urge to confront the other woman. That's what the next chapter is all about.

the other woman and the love triangle: smart moves/ dumb moves

Many betrayed wives feel an impulsive urge to confront the other woman. They hope to scare her, intimidate her, or convince her to "Leave my husband alone!" For some, it is a passing thought. For others it's an obsession—particularly when the other woman persists in contacting the man and keeping the affair alive. There are times when confronting the other woman may be helpful. More often than not it only complicates the situation. But you can weaken the love triangle without directly attacking the other woman.

Even if you have no desire to confront the other woman, this chapter will provide more clues as to what makes you tick and what keeps love triangles operating long after they should have disintegrated. Your real power comes from within—understanding yourself and your situation—so you can make sound choices and operate from personal integrity. (Unless you wish to save your marriage but lose yourself in the process.)

Emotional Triangles

A "love triangle" is a common term used to describe an affair. Then the drama unfolds: secrecy followed by exposure followed by the push-pull of competing desires—and all of the emotional damage (usually extensive) that results.

Step back from the concept of "love triangles" and look instead at what therapists call "emotional triangles." A love triangle is a special kind of emotional triangle. But all emotional triangles operate according to a certain set of rules. If you understand those rules, you will know what steps to take. If you do not understand the rules, you will probably make your situation worse. (When it comes to dealing with emotional triangles, ignorance is not bliss.) There are five main rules you need to understand about emotional triangles:

1. They form when the anxiety or tension between two people gets too high.
2. They tend to make underlying problems persist, not change.
3. At any moment in time, two people in the triangle are more connected and the other is on the outside.
4. Trying to directly force the other two people in the triangle to break up usually strengthens their bond.
5. If you try and fail to break up the other two, you will take on more of their stress and they will feel more at ease.

They Form When the Anxiety or Tension Between Two People Gets Too High

Emotional triangles exist everywhere in your life. A triangle forms when the level of anxiety (distress, discomfort, unease, pain, and so forth) between two people rises to a tipping point for at least one of those persons. Then that person "triangles in" a third person (or thing or issue) in order to reduce anxiety. For example, imagine you are at a cocktail party chatting uneasily with a stranger and wish to end the conversation but don't know how to do it gracefully. Your discomfort level rises and then you might say, "My goodness, there's Jane. I haven't seen her in years. Jane, come over here!" Now Jane gets drawn into your two-person interaction in order to reduce your anxiety.

Triangles Tend to Make Underlying Problems Persist, Not Change

A common triangle in marriages (when the couple is low on intimacy and wishes to avoid dealing directly with that issue) is for one spouse to focus more attention on the children or for a spouse to focus extra attention on work (or on stress relievers such as TV, the Internet, or alcohol). Therefore, when a couple at home is feeling uncomfortable with each other or may in fact be arguing, one spouse can say, "I need to give the kids their bath" or "I have some work to do on the computer" as a way to alleviate strain.

The problem with such maneuvers is that it puts the troubled relationship on hold and no issues get solved. *When triangles are in operation, issues don't get resolved—they get reshelved.* When there is high anxiety in a relationship, there are three options. You can confront the issues head-on with all of the anxiety that goes along with doing so; you can end the relationship; or you can divert attention away from the problematic issues by focusing on some other issue, person, or thing. If diversion is repeatedly chosen, nothing is changed and the status quo is maintained.

Two People in the Triangle Are More Connected and the Other Is on the Outside

Who is "in" and who is "out" can shift. For example, imagine John and Mary have a troubled marriage. Mary helps cope with her anxiety by seeking her mother's advice. Her mother knows many of the couple's problems and may or may not take sides. If the advice Mary receives helps her to go to John and all is resolved, fine. But if their marital problems recur and she keeps talking to her mother about them, then an emotional triangle has formed. When Mary and her Mom are united, John is on the outside. If John complains to Mary that his mother-in-law is too involved and Mary agrees, now Mary and John are more united and the mother is on the outside. If the mother-in-law thinks Mary is unreasonable and calls John to offer emotional support, she and John are united and Mary is on the outside.

Sometimes there is no shifting of roles. One person is always on the outside and the other two are much closer. This situation ensures that no real change will occur unless one person opts out of the triangle.

Forcing the Other Two People in the Triangle to Break Up Strengthens Their Bond

The other two are connected precisely because one is in conflict with you. His anxiety is reduced by connecting to the third person. If you are in conflict with someone who has triangled in a third party, using force to pry them apart is like trying to take a bone away from a hungry dog. They will usually unite to strengthen their bond. This is true whether you are trying to break up a spouse and his lover, an addict and her habit, or a child and his favorite toy.

If You Fail to Break Up the Other Two, You Will Take on More Stress

As the other two unite, their stress decreases. You will become more frustrated and insecure. Less anxious people have no strong desire to change their situation. Their motivation to change decreases. But your motivation to change them *increases* and yet you have the least power. (Who is usually more stressed and least in control, the wife who repeatedly tries and fails to get her alcoholic husband to stop drinking? Or the husband who finds more clever ways to hide his liquor and still abuse alcohol?)

So you can see that a simple idea of "confronting the other woman" is not so simple after all. It may not only fail, but it may draw them closer together and ease their anxiety while intensifying yours. Not a smart move.

Three's a Crowd—Don't Make It a Circus

It's time to take a closer look at your particular situation and determine what course of action, if any, you should take regarding the other woman. There are four broad areas to consider:

1. What is (was) the nature of the affair and degree of overall threat to your relationship?
2. How did he feel about himself in the affair?
3. What are your truest motivations for confronting her?
4. Given the above, what are the likely consequences?

The Nature of the Affair

There are basically four types of affairs. His affair was brief (one-night stand) or longer but was for sex only; his affair was online only (no physical connection, no meeting for lunch); his affair was emotional with no sex; his affair was emotional and sexual.

All affairs can threaten a relationship. A one-night stand with a stranger after getting drunk at a bar can crush a marriage as easily as a long-term emotionally involved affair can. However, on average, the less emotional investment a man has in his affair partner, the greater the likelihood he will want the marriage to survive. The longer the affair continues, the harder it will be for him to end it. The more emotionally connected he felt, the more likely he will carry "feelings" for her for some time to come.

Recommendations

- If the affair was a one-night stand with a stranger with no emotional attachment, don't try to seek out the other woman and confront her. She poses no threat. But confronting her could lead to unexpected dangers or complications.

- If the affair was online and the woman does not reside nearby, it's probably okay (but unnecessary) to send her a note stating your anger and your decision to work on the marriage. **Avoid any language that can be interpreted as threatening.** (You may feel powerful when you vent like that, but you may also be arrested.) Better to ignore her.

- If the affair was emotional and/or sexual, the other woman likely has feelings for your husband (and he for her). If she happens to be a friend or a relative of yours, you already have a relationship with her and confronting her makes sense but will probably not be satisfying. You may have a little more leverage since, being a friend or family member, you can make her personal life much more complicated depending upon whom you choose to inform about the betrayal. Still, the fact that your husband betrayed you with someone from your inner circle suggests that relationship and personal problems run far deeper for everyone involved.

Confronting may or may not help but don't make her your priority. She isn't trustworthy. Anything she tells you is suspect. And if she is bold enough to have an affair with your husband while being your friend or relative, she may not care about consequences to the affair being exposed within the family or friendship circles.

How Did He Feel about Himself in the Affair?

Was he her knight in shining armor? Did he feel he was rescuing her (perhaps from an abusive husband or other stressful situation)? If so, your confronting her will tug at his heartstrings—for her. He will want to protect her—from you. You will be shining a light on the very quality that attracted him to her (she was a victim, he was her hero). Don't do it.

Did he feel cared about by her? Listened to? Appreciated? Then he will view her as a good person who does not deserve to be verbally attacked. He will claim (truthfully) that he is responsible for his past choices and that the other woman is not responsible for his actions. He will view your attack on her as malicious, immature, and unnecessary, and as evidence that once again you do not understand or appreciate his side of things. Don't do it.

Was the other woman the "calm in the center of a storm" for him? In other words, was she a sanctuary from the stresses of his life? He will regard your desire to confront her as adding more stress to his life and he will pull away from you. Don't do it.

Was the other woman simply a toy for him to play with? Did he use her? Did she fulfill his narcissistic need for admiration? If so, he may not care if you confront her or not. But you have bigger problems on your hands. Your man is much more interested in his needs and focusing on what he feels entitled to than on looking honestly at the marriage and at what you require. Ignore her—she probably has enough problems in her life—and look more closely at whether or not you can really stay with a man like him.

What Are Your Truest Motivations for Confronting Her?

Be honest. If it is to attack, intimidate, or punish her, that is extremely understandable but extremely risky. At best you will feel a bit better for venting but you will change nothing. You may even make the situation worse.

Is it to protect your marriage? That's a fine motive. But will it work? If the other woman has no idea you exist and would never be involved with a married man and has been lied to by your husband, she may appreciate knowing those facts. If that is the case, she is as much a victim as you are. Go easy on her. She may become your ally. But if the other woman is heavily invested in maintaining a relationship with your husband, your words will fall on deaf ears. You may give her more information about yourself that she can use to manipulate you. Better avoid this conversation.

Is your motivation to gain a clearer understanding of all that has happened? Do you simply wish to clarify matters and not attack her? That is a more reasonable motivation—if you can handle what she may tell you. But you may not know for sure if what she tells you is the truth. If she wants to keep your husband, she may tell you things to make you more furious with him, whether or not they're true.

Is your motivation "I'll just feel better if I confront the bitch!"? Be very, very careful. If the other woman still tries to contact your husband, even in small "innocent" ways, you'll regard it as a slap in your face. You may become outraged at her gall and insist that your husband tell her off in ways he will never feel comfortable doing. Or, if they happen to work with each other, you'll be fuming if the other woman so much as tells him to "have a nice day" since you'll see it as her way of being passive-aggressive against you.

Given All of the Above, What Are the Likely Consequences?

If you wish to save your marriage, there is a small chance that confronting the other woman will result in her pulling away from your man. (However, that in no way pulls him toward you—he may be out of the affair but still emotionally out of the marriage, too.) I have spoken to women who have confronted the other woman and who believed it helped, but most didn't. Most said it aggravated the situation or at best accomplished nothing. Some wives got into serious legal troubles by confronting the other woman.

If the affair is ongoing or has a chance of reigniting (or if your husband has feelings for her even though the affair is clearly over and done with), then any negative attack you make on the other woman (or even *about* her) will result in your husband drawing emotionally closer to her. At a minimum he will feel sorry for her—when he should be feeling sorry for you. If the affair has a chance of reigniting, you can bet that the other woman will contact your husband, inform him of the awful things you said, feel victimized by you, and tug on his heartstrings.

Should You Contact the Other Woman's Husband or Boyfriend?

If the woman your husband has been having an affair with is married, you may have contemplated informing her husband. You need to ask the question "Will that draw my husband and her closer together?" No way to tell for sure. Affairs are often fed by the drama that unfolds when the affair is exposed. Then it becomes "them" against "you." If your desire is to complicate her life, you will succeed. But it may hinder your chances of reconciling with your husband, especially if he views what you did as vicious.

The bottom line: if the other woman is already out of the picture, don't bring her back in by confronting her. If she is still in the picture, your husband has the power to end the affair, not you. Don't risk drawing them closer.

Can the Triangle Be Dismantled?

Yes. But you must run the risk that you will be the odd woman out. Triangles persist because of the cooperation of all three individuals. If any one of you said, "I'm done with this!" and meant it, the triangle would fall apart. Obviously, if you still want your marriage to succeed, you're hoping the other woman will leave or your husband will end the affair. Then there is no triangle, just two people (you and him) trying to rebuild. But what if one of them has mixed feelings? That is the most common scenario I witness as a therapist. She pulls away, then recontacts him. Or he says the affair is over but secretly calls her "just to talk." In those cases, their relationship will be kept in balance (or not) by *your* actions, too. If you try to pull them apart or convince him to end the affair, he will automatically be drawn toward her at least emotionally. (As a silly but common example, imagine you wish to buy a blouse. You find one that is perfect but is more expensive than you'd like. And there is only one like it on the rack. As you struggle to make a decision, another woman sees the blouse, exclaims "I love this!" and takes it from the rack. Now, what are your feelings toward the blouse? You *want* it. When anyone has strong mixed feelings—especially about something important—and someone else tries to prevent them from having one side of it, the other side usually becomes more attractive.)

So what do you do? You have two major steps to take if it is possible for the triangle to fall apart.

1. **You must only try to change the relationship you are in.** That means focus solely on your relationship with your husband. Don't direct your energy unwisely toward the other woman and don't try to force (persuade, cajole, manipulate, coerce, and so on) your husband to abandon his relationship with her. You are not "in" that relationship. He must abandon it because he wants to, not because you forced it.

2. **You must reverse the polarity of anxiety.** In other words, if you are more anxious about his affair and of the possibility of losing the marriage than he is, you have less power and he has less mo-

tivation to make changes. (The person who is unsure if he or she wants the relationship to work always has more power and more leverage in the relationship than the person who is sure.) If the marriage is to survive and thrive, you must not be more invested in things working out than he is. That means you may have to emotionally detach somewhat and be willing to *accept* that the marriage might not work out. In order to do that, you have to find inner resources of strength, feel less emotionally dependent, and be willing to let the chips fall where they may. For things to improve, he has to be worried and anxious about losing *you* at least as much as you're afraid of losing him.

One way to reverse the polarity is by maintaining healthy emotional boundaries. I guarantee that if you are floundering in your effort to manage the painful effects of an affair, your boundaries are out of whack.

Love Knows No Boundaries—or Does It?

For someone to love you, truly love *you*, and be devoted to the relationship in a mature way, there must be a "you" to love. The problem for many is that they lose sight of themselves in a relationship. While men often shield themselves somewhat from closeness to preserve a sense of self, women often enter into a relationship to further fulfill themselves. In other words, they become more dependent upon the relationship succeeding in order to feel worthwhile.

A healthy person has emotional boundaries that allow good things in and keep bad things out. So someone who worries about being liked or "What do people think of me?" may say yes to things when she should say no. She may tolerate an inadequate or abusive relationship. Think of the cells in your body. They have walls that allow nutrients or hormones in but that try to keep viruses or bacteria out. A weak immune system lets in too many invaders. Or it cannot distinguish between invaders and itself so it attacks itself (which is what happens with arthritis, lupus, or autoimmune diseases). A weak immune system underreacts to danger (an infection that does not heal) or overreacts (an allergy). If your husband had an affair and you are desperate for the marriage to survive, your emotional immune system may go into overdrive. If so, you will overfunction (be suspicious, attacking, obsessed) and try to control things you cannot control (the other woman, his whereabouts) while not controlling well what you might control (your own emotional reaction). The weaker your own emotional immune system, the more you need to be protected from the outside (or put a bubble around your relationship—very impractical) in order to thrive. That is not in your best interests.

To strengthen your emotional immune system and have healthy boundaries, you must define what you will do and not do, what you will tolerate or not tolerate. You must make choices and not be indecisive or wavering. The focus is on *your* response to adversity, not on how others (your husband and "the other woman") should respond.

So, for example, you cannot really control whether your husband is still seeing the other woman in secret. But you can say, *"I am willing to work with you and rebuild our relationship. However, if I am of the opinion you are not fully committed to me, I will reconsider whether I will stay with you."* That takes the pressure off of you to try to "catch him" in a lie. It puts the pressure on him. Unless he can convince you that he is not still involved with the other woman, you may leave him.

By defining yourself you need to come up with a "bottom line." This is a statement of integrity, not one of threat or manipulation. Is your bottom line that you will never under any circumstances leave your husband (due to financial concerns, the children, religious beliefs, or lack of confidence in yourself to cope)? Or would you do so under a certain set of conditions? If so, what are those conditions? How long will you allow yourself to be abused, humiliated, lied to, or toyed with? Stating your bottom line does not guarantee that your husband will cooperate. That is not the purpose. This is not about "getting" him to fall in line. It is about clarifying where you stand so that you can make a decision what to do next. It is about you and only you, not him. If he is convinced that you are willing to end a marriage if it becomes unworkable for you, and he wants the marriage to survive more than he wants it to fail, he will now move *toward* you. If, on the other hand, he sees you as being desperate or wishy-washy, he can afford to move slowly and possibly move *away* from you.

Abandon Any Desire for Drama

If you are having a difficult time detaching from the emotional triangle (that is, not getting caught up in the emotional whirlwind it creates) you are too busy creating stories in your mind or replaying the same old stories. You are caught up in (at least) four mind games:

1. "What if?"
2. "I'm a victim."

3. "I'm entitled to rage."
4. "Life is so unfair!"

If you worry about future possibilities that cannot be fully answered at this moment in time, such as your financial situation, the impact of a divorce on your children, or the likelihood of finding a new mate and being happy ("What if?"); or if you chew over details on how you've been betrayed, lied to, or humiliated, ("I'm a victim"); or if you obsess over ways to get even and feel it is your right to keep attacking your partner or the other woman ("I'm entitled to rage"); or if you brood over how you didn't deserve what happened ("Life is so unfair!"), there will be only one outcome for you: a state of helplessness and misery.

Change Mind Games into Mind Frames

Those four mind games are very common. They represent the human condition that arises when fear takes over. But in order to get out of the emotional triangle you are in, they must be replaced by four *mind frames*:

1. "What if" is replaced by "I accept . . ." That is to be followed by any statement that makes sense *in this present moment* such as:

   "I accept that I am afraid of my future and *I accept that I cannot fully know my future right now* and *that things may turn out well."*

   "I accept that I am worried about my children's welfare and *I accept that I will do all I can to help them."*

128

"I accept that money may be tight if we divorce and *I accept that I will not be destitute and will have resources available to help me."*

As you recall from Chapter 4, acceptance allows you to peacefully coexist with conflicting thoughts, without trying to solve what cannot be solved in the moment. It eliminates the inner struggle to come up with answers when none can be had.

2. "I'm a victim" is replaced by "I accept that I am hurt **and** that I am in charge of my life . . . I can make choices that will help me . . . I can ask for help."

3. "I'm entitled to rage" is replaced by "I'm entitled to speak my mind without harming others . . . I'm entitled to peace of mind and a life of integrity . . . I'm entitled to the love of those who truly care for me."

4. "Life is so unfair" is replaced by "I am so unfair to myself when I demand that others change in order for me to be happy." Or "I accept that life is unfair **and** I accept that sometimes it is fair."

Checklist for De-Triangling

Answer Yes or No to the following statements to the extent the statements are true for you now.

1. I can stop focusing on the other woman and focus instead on my relationship with my husband.

2. I can stop trying to force him to stay away from her.

3. I can see my deeper motivations for wanting to confront her.

4. I can contemplate the probable consequences if I confront her.

5. I can feel pain (hurt, anger, sadness, fear) without it turning into drama (hysteria, rage, paranoia, depression, and panic).

6. I can define clearly how *I* feel, what *I* want, what *I* will and will not put up with rather than obsess about what *he* must do or not do.

7. I can imagine a decent life without him in it even if I don't want that to happen.

8. If the marriage ends I can manage.

9. I am willing to work within the marriage to try and save it, if he is also willing.

10. I can stop viewing myself as a victim, stop obsessing that I didn't deserve this, stop worrying about matters I can do nothing about at this present moment.

There is no score. The more items you can respond Yes to, the greater likelihood you will not be emotionally devastated by the "love triangle" and the more healthy will be your emotional boundaries.

ten

conversations

you're almost

guaranteed

to have

Talking may stop and start but communication never ends. Somehow, some way, you two will be sending messages to each other. The more clear, direct, aboveboard, and less hostile the better. In the roller coaster phase your conversations will be intense and unsettling, but the sooner you improve them the sooner you can get to productive discussions.

In the subdued phase, intense conversations will be less frequent but there will be gaps of quiet unhappiness. Most of the fighting will have dissipated. Conversations can still be stilted as each of you walks on eggshells and feels that you can't really be yourself. In the rebuilding phase your conversations are lighter, brighter, and more focused on your future than your past. But even when you think you may be making conversational headway there are numerous landmines that can throw you off course. If you manage them well, the odds of healing your wounds and strengthening the relationship can vastly increase.

Your life isn't in freeze-frame after the affair. You're still working and raising the kids; perhaps your extended family is aware of what's happened and they are concerned; the other woman may not be entirely out of the picture. You struggle to feel more connected to the spouse who betrayed you. You both move gingerly around each other. A nice evening together may be followed by emotional distance the next day. Nothing feels normal.

As the weeks progress there are conversations that you may not be expecting to have but that commonly occur. These can become "mini-crises" if mishandled. In addition to keeping in mind the SAIL method, use these tips:

- Don't get hung up on one or two words your spouse uses. Go with the spirit of what's being said. For example, if he says you "always" find fault with him, don't get stuck on the word "always" if what he really means is "You find fault with me more than I think is fair." Similarly, if he uses a certain word in one sentence but uses a variation of that word in the next, don't pounce on him for being inconsistent. Ask yourself, "Do I know what he is really trying to say?" If you don't, ask for clarification. If you do, cut him slack.

- During difficult conversations, avoid reminding him, "If you never cheated we wouldn't be going through this right now."

- Report your feelings, don't demonstrate them. Saying "I feel worried every time you leave for work" is much different (and more effective) than angrily accusing him of wanting to spend time with "her" every time he leaves for work.

- Take a few seconds to get your thoughts together before responding any time your spouse says something provocative, unkind, or unexpected.

- Limit or postpone conversations if you are overtired, too angry, or too stressed by other matters.

- If you want him to be up front, don't punish honesty.

- Speak concisely, no long-winded speeches. Otherwise his anxiety will shoot up, he'll speak *less*, and the conversation will be a disappointment.

- Focus more on areas of agreement that you can build upon instead of hammering those areas where you don't agree.

- If he uses humor during a serious conversation, view it as his way to keep his emotions under control, not as a sign he's not taking things seriously.

- Don't keep repeating yourself; he'll feel nagged or talked down to. If you don't think he "gets it," ask him to clarify what he does understand and correct any misunderstandings.

These ten conversations may occur anytime, any place. Better to be prepared.

Conversation #1

Scenario: Weeks or months have passed since the exposure of the affair. Suddenly he reveals "new" information you didn't know before. Perhaps he admits to a lie and now corrects it, or unintentionally reveals something he'd been keeping a secret. Now you wonder, "Why didn't you tell me this before? What else are you hiding?!"

The deeper concern is his trustworthiness. If the new information is a bit of minor data (during the affair he had lunch with her at a restaurant he'd forgotten to mention even though he'd mentioned all the others) don't react as if it were much bigger news (he'd gotten her pregnant and never bothered to tell you). Try to get some perspective. Does the new information really change anything about your goals and how you view him? What were his reasons for not revealing the information sooner? Was it unimportant data to him? Or was he afraid that if you found out you'd leave him? And why is he telling you now? Was it by accident? Did he do so purposely because he felt you should know but hadn't found the right time until now?

New information often results in a setback for the couple because it stokes your worries that he is still keeping secrets. This might open up a whole new round of discussions where you go over details you'd gone over dozens of times before—wondering if he'll keep his story straight. Unless the new information is earth-shattering, it's best to limit the amount of time you focus on the new information and what it means. No more than a few days is desirable. While progress in the relationship has many ups and downs, you don't want to go back to square one. Best to say something like "I'm glad you told me. But my trust in you has now fallen a little. It's essential that you be completely up front and honest about everything. If I cannot trust you significantly more than I now do, this marriage will not work."

Your goal is to make him more worried about losing you than you are worried about losing him. Battering him with more questions reveals that you are highly anxious. You don't need to have all the answers you think you need. You just need to believe that he is sincerely remorseful and wants to heal this relationship. If that's true, then you'll handle it if new information is revealed. However, if new information keeps cropping up every so often when he had promised he'd already told you everything, serious questions about his truthfulness must be raised.

Conversation #2

Scenario: The memory of the affair is triggered in a big way when the two of you are watching a movie where someone cheats or are reading about a celebrity affair.

Talk about a mood-killer. Affairs are everywhere. You can't read a magazine or turn on the TV without being reminded of your husband's infidelity. Inevitably you'll be reminded precisely at a time you and he are finally having some pleasant moments together. At those moments your head might be saying, "Try not to let it bother me" but your heart has already sunk and you feel unhappy.

In an ideal situation, your husband would speak up. He'd let you know he feels bad for you at that moment and try to reassure you of his devotion. But that doesn't usually happen. He may be afraid to say anything and just hope that somehow you'll overlook it. Or maybe he is still awash in mixed emotions and can't say anything to you with enough conviction that you believe him. So you end up showing him how pained you now feel.

An ineffective conversation might go like this:

You: I can't even enjoy a movie without being reminded about what you did.

Him: Don't let it get to you.

You: Easy for you to say.

Him: I'm just saying we have to stay on track and not get sidetracked by any reminders.

You: You don't get it. A reminder isn't a small thing. It hurts. A *lot*. You just want me to minimize things so you can feel better. I still don't think my feelings are as important to you.

Him: Why are you starting an argument? Can't you put things in the past for at least a couple of hours?

In this exchange, your feelings and opinions make perfect sense. The problem is twofold: you made an accusatory opening comment, and he missed an opportunity to show sensitivity and caring.

A better conversation might sound like this:

You (reporting what you feel): When I see scenes like that on TV I still get that feeling in the pit of my stomach.

Him: Don't let it get to you.

You: What I'd like right now is for you to understand what I'm feeling and maybe to offer some reassurance.

Him: Haven't I been reassuring?

You: And the more often you do it the better I feel. This won't be the first movie we watch where someone's having an affair. I'd like you to reach out to me at those times and not freeze up.

Again, in an ideal situation you wouldn't have to spell it out for him. But unfortunately you may have to ask for what you want very explicitly. Chances are he's afraid to do anything that will upset the apple cart so his default response will be to do nothing (a head-in-the-sand approach).

Conversation #3

Scenario: You insist on knowing all of the sexually explicit details of the affair—and he is reluctant to divulge them.

Some people get obsessed with knowing sexual details. They convince themselves that their imagination is worse than the reality and that knowing for sure what happened would put their minds at ease. I've rarely found it to be helpful for a betrayed partner to learn explicit details. The images, since they are true and not imagination, play more vividly in your mind—usually when you'd rather be asleep. If you have insecurities about your appearance, your body, your attractiveness, or your sexual prowess, then this wreaks havoc with your self-esteem and your ability to get past the images. Yes, it's important to know if there were any unsafe sex practices, but that might be all you need to know. Sometimes the need to know about graphic sexual details is really a search to answer a different question.

- Am I attractive and appealing enough sexually to him (and others)?
- Am I mostly bothered by the fact that he doesn't want to tell me details (he's being secretive again) than I am about the need to know the details?
- Do I feel out of control when I don't have answers—any answers—so I must keep harping on an issue even if it's to my detriment to do so?

If an honest self-assessment reveals that one of the above reasons is what's driving your desire for graphic details, it's better to find other ways to examine those issues. Knowing sexually graphic details will not really help you.

However, if you insist on knowing the gory details it is probably best if your husband cooperates. His refusal will feel like another wall between you. Chances are it will make you feel worse but at least you won't be able to accuse him of not cooperating or of harboring sensual secrets. But be prepared. If you don't like what you are hearing remember that you asked for it. Punishing him for being honest is not to your ultimate advantage. I suggest you choose your questions carefully, start with something less provocative and work your way up. The moment you realize that you heard an answer you'd rather not have heard it might be time to stop the discussion. For example, Tina first asked her husband questions about the romantic setting. *Did you have wine or champagne? Was it a small motel room or a well-adorned hotel?* Then she asked more about the sexual acts. *Was she wild in bed or somewhat reserved? Is she in better shape than me? Did you prefer her breasts to mine? Did you make love for hours or was it over quickly? Did she have orgasms?* When the topic of oral sex came to Tina's mind, she grew increasingly uncomfortable and wasn't sure she wanted to know the answer. She decided to stop at that point.

The best thing to do is to give it more time before demanding answers and see if you still feel a strong need to have those questions answered six months from now. Chances are you won't. And you'll be better off for it.

Conversation #4

Scenario: A large celebration is planned with your family. They know all about his affair. He doesn't want to attend because he will feel self-conscious. You think he has to break the ice eventually and now is as good a time as any. Also, he's annoyed that you told your family so many details about his affair to begin with.

If the level of anger or animosity between you two is still high, it's best that he not attend. If you'll have a hard time remaining friendly at the gathering, better to wait until your relationship has improved before you enter into such an awkward, stressful situation. But if your relationship is less inflamed and you both seem squarely on the side of reconciliation, it's in everyone's best interest if he attends the gathering. The first time he gets together with your family will feel awkward no matter what. In the conversation you have with him about going to the gathering you may want to focus on the "L" in SAIL. That is, what are you each willing to do to help address mutual concerns? For example, he may agree to attend and visit with your family days or weeks ahead of time to break the ice earlier (or speak to them on the phone). You might agree to stand by his side frequently, smile at him more, and indicate to others by your actions that you two are on the mend. Or you might speak to your family ahead of time and ask that they support your efforts at reconciliation by being as welcoming as possible to your husband despite their personal feelings.

Look at Me While I'm Talking to You!

Women usually prefer eye contact when conversing. However, under stressful conditions or when the woman is very emotional, *men are not at all comfortable with eye contact.* When he doesn't look at you during these conversations, it isn't necessarily because he doesn't care. It's probably because he is overwhelmed and anxious. He avoids looking you in the eye as a way to manage (lower) his own emotions. If you can speak slowly, respectfully, and with not much emotional upset you'll discover he can look you in the eye more easily.

If his main issue is anger that you divulged personal information to your family, not attending a gathering is not a solution. He may have a point: if your family is now aligned against him it just makes the entire situation hard to deal with. Best to admit that each of you had needs that were incompatible: you needed to get support from your family during the affair crisis while he needed to keep the problems as a private matter. Just as he wants you to some day "get over" the affair, he will need to get over the fact that your family knows a lot about the details of your marriage.

Conversation #5

Scenario: Your children show signs of distress in the aftermath of the affair. You blame him. He blames your inability to be forgiving as the main reason for their upset.

One of two things is going on with him. Either he's blaming you because he has yet to accept responsibility for his affair (not a good sign) or he is frustrated and worried he'll never get out from under his huge mistake. If it's the latter, he's really asking you to stop hitting him over the head with what happened and to approach the issue with the children in a cooperative, non-blaming way. He's weary of the conflict.

The best approach is for each of you to respond to the question "What is it I need my partner to understand that I don't think he (she) understands?" (That is the "I" in SAIL—what's important?) Once that understanding is reached, go directly to the "L" in SAIL and list what you are each willing to do about the issue. For example, you might say, "I need you to understand that I shouldn't be criticized for struggling to forgive you." He might say, "I need you to understand that our kids are affected by how well or how poorly we get along." Based on that understanding you come up with a plan that might include the two of you talking to the children together and reassuring them that the marriage is being worked on and there are no plans to break up. (If breaking up is a real possibility, tell the children you are doing all you can to repair the marriage and leave it at that for now.)

Conversation #6

Scenario: You plan a romantic getaway with your husband to help rebuild the closeness. But your heart isn't in it and he's annoyed that you're not trying hard to make the best of things.

This issue is a stand-in for a larger issue: he wants to make progress as quickly as possible and put the ugly past behind him while you need more time. You're not to blame if a romantic getaway doesn't carry the excitement it used to. You're afraid that if you get all enthusiastic about a trip together he'll regard his affair as a minor bump in the road. Acceptance (the "A" in SAIL) goes a long way here. You need to accept the fact that he is eager to make significant strides in moving past the affair, and he needs to accept that his betrayal hurt you deeply and will affect your level of passion for him. Your goal on the getaway is to make the best of it. But let him know "If I'm having a good time it doesn't mean all is forgiven and forgotten. And if I'm not having a good time, it doesn't mean I don't want us to be happier together. Just bear with me." In other words, give each other permission to feel what you each feel and don't get into a debate over how one "should" be feeling. As a rule of thumb, whenever one of you has strong mixed feelings it makes no sense to try to talk yourself out of one side of those feelings. Both sides must be honored, for now anyway, since that is how you feel.

Conversation #7

Scenario: It seems that whenever you're preoccupied about his affair you have to be the one to bring it up. You wish he would raise the issue once in a while so you don't always feel like a nag or the "bad guy."

Months may have gone by since the affair ended, and while you have good days you also have many not-so-good days. You feel out of sorts and you know why. He knows why, too. But rather than come up to you and give you a hug or remind you he's sorry, he avoids you. So then you get snippy with him. Instead of taking the hint he gives you a wide berth. If you finally complain to him that he's so standoffish when "you must know how I've been feeling" he'll get defensive and say that you should have said something earlier. You wonder, where is his sensitivity?

Chances are he is not as insensitive as you think. But he's operating from a typical male instinct. If he was with his buddies and one of them was going through a very rough personal time, his pals would probably give him space and wait for him to bring up the subject. By not raising the topic for him, they are really communicating to him "We have faith you can handle this but we're here if you need us." (They also do it that way because they are uneasy when others' emotions are raw.)

If he truly wants the marriage to succeed and he has shown in other ways that he cares about how you feel, then he needs to be explicitly told what you want from him—and probably reminded of it. Tell him, "If you can tell I'm preoccupied or look sad I need you to come up to me and ask what's wrong. If I say 'Nothing' I'd still appreciate it if you'd use that as an opportunity to reassure me of how you feel about me. I don't want to be the one who always has to bring up the fact that I'm still hurting over your affair."

Conversation #8

Scenario: He complains that "You keep throwing the past in my face."

Believe me, if you'd had an affair and he was the injured party he wouldn't be arguing that the two of you must "get over it" and "focus on the future rather than the past." He'd be reminding you almost daily of what you did that was so horribly wrong. Why? Because men are more comfortable with their anger and sense of entitlement. They are not at all comfortable with their emotions of guilt, sadness, or fear. So when you are the one who was deeply hurt—and he knows he is responsible—he can't sit with his uncomfortable feelings for long. He needs to know he is redeemed. Therefore he'll get angry with you for bringing up his affair because he cannot easily regulate his own internal discomfort when you do so. He needs to escape the situation to feel better and your reminders of what happened make it impossible for him to do so. That doesn't mean you must go along with his wishes in this regard. But it helps to understand why he acts that way.

Before you have this conversation, ask yourself if in fact you bring up the past simply to punish him. If so, that won't help—even though your motives are understandable. Usually when people bring up the past again and again it's because they don't feel the listener fully understands the suffering that's been endured. Or something is happening now that reminds the person of a past hurt. For example, let's say he goes out for two hours. You ask him where he went. He says he went to the hardware store. Later you learn he also went to the gas station and stopped off for a take-out coffee. You get annoyed with him for not telling you "the whole truth" and say it reminds you of how he kept secrets from you when he was having an affair. Now he gets angry that you keep bringing up the affair and are making a big deal over the fact that he stopped for gasoline. The issue there is not so much the affair but that any information that's withheld or any form of half-truth, however innocent, will trigger a wave of painful memories. He needs to understand that and be more willing to give you more details (however minor) next time.

In conversation about this issue, it's best if you let him know you will be more aware of when you bring up the past and that you won't do so without some forethought. Ideally he will then be more patient.

Conversation #9

Scenario: The other woman, who perhaps works with your husband, still makes herself known to him even in casual, small-talk ways. She says things like "Don't tell your wife we spoke." He tells you anyway (good for him) but now you insist he tell her off and refuse to have anything to do with her ever again under any circumstances. He resists and accuses you of overreacting.

If he is encouraging interactions with the other woman, you have a problem. If he is doing his hardest to steer clear of her but cannot control her actions, he will probably take exception to any request you make of him that is way out of his comfort zone. Just as he hates to be in conflict with you, he hates to be in conflict with her, too. He'd rather ignore her as much as possible and hope she fades into the background. Asking him to yell at her or intimidate her "to prove to me that you care more about my feelings than hers" will backfire. (One woman I counseled was strolling through the mall with her husband when she spotted the "other woman" walking with friends. The wife insisted that her husband go to the woman and loudly call her a "whore" in front of her friends. When he refused, it set their relationship back for months. That was *not* a wise request on the wife's part.)

Your trust of him must, ultimately, be a leap of faith. Giving him over-the-top tests to pass will harm your efforts to reconcile. Better to ignore the other woman and ask that your husband report to you any encounters he has with her. And thank him for being up-front and honest about those encounters.

Conversation #10

Scenario: One apology isn't enough. You aren't sure how often he should apologize but you resent it when he gets irritated and claims, "I've apologized several times already! How many times do I have to repeat it!?"

Hopefully, he has apologized—more than once. But there comes a point where his remorse and regret will not be obvious from his words but from his actions. Many men convey their apologies through activities such as helping out more, making home repairs the woman wants, buying gifts, and so forth. He hopes you pick up on his sincere remorse without him having to repeat it verbally. Why is he so averse to saying "I'm sorry" many times? First, he will resist saying it if you

146

demand it because he realizes it won't be accepted as sincere once you have to remind him to do it. Second, an apology is viewed by men as the initial step toward reconciliation. Once they've apologized they're ready to move forward. Requesting another apology appears to men as if the two of you have reversed direction. Finally, when men apologize they don't want to belabor the point. They hope you accept it and let it be. But many women, once their men apologize, feel a need to further discuss what happened and why the apology was necessary. Anticipating that another apology will just open up the discussion to rehash the past, they resist saying they are sorry.

If you have a discussion about the need for more apologies, keep it simple. Let him know that his apologies help you feel reassured and do not imply there was something lacking about his past apologies. Let him know you won't belabor the issue if he does apologize or punish him if he resists. But it's important he try to offer you periodic reassurances, *in his own way*, that remind you he cares about the impact of his affair on you.

As time moves on you will feel drained but perhaps more hopeful. Additional coping strategies can help. That's what the next chapter offers.

mental and emotional fatigue: more coping strategies

You are in the subdued phase. Time has passed—perhaps several months—since the affair became known. If you have decided to try to work things out you have probably reached a stage of exhaustion. For you, anger, hurt, and mistrust are still present. But the feelings have dulled a bit and hopefully there has been reason for optimism. The strain has had a toll on him, too. He may want the marriage to work out but perhaps is secretly unsure if you'll ever be happy again and he is weary of the battle. The goal now is to hang in there and not make the situation worse.

Your Highest Level of Consciousness

If you choose to look behind you at what you've been put through, the subdued phase can be a dismal stage. However, if you look ahead you may see a light at the end of the tunnel. The light is still far off—it will be some time before you can feel whole again—but your journey has overcome the roughest spots. Yes, you and your husband must continue to heal and improve the relationship—that's "outer" work. And if you've decided to separate you must manage the practical aspects of your life—also outer work. But at this juncture you will find it helpful to do more "inner" work. After all, it's your inner life that is the funnel through which everything that happens to you gets processed.

Until now you've probably been operating mostly in survival mode. Higher qualities of life—beauty, art, profound love, and so on—have escaped you. You're simply trying to get through each day without collapsing. Survival mode means you're under attack or being threatened. Stress hormones pulse through your body and you remain on edge, unable to completely feel at ease. In survival mode it's "Do or die." As long as you remain in that mode you cannot be happy or at peace.

Levels of Happiness

What makes you happy? An infant is happy when it gets its immediate needs met. So are we. We feel happy when we buy things we really want. Immediate gratification ("I'm hungry—let's eat!") fulfills us and makes us happy or content—but only for a very brief time. Then we need more and more immediate gratification to sustain our happiness. A toddler is happy not just when he is fed or has a toy but when he accomplishes something such as learning to walk or eat with a spoon. Adults feel happy when they accomplish things they set out to do. We can also feel happy when we extend ourselves for others in a loving way. We give gifts and our only reward is the smile on the other person's face, for example.

Dr. Robert Spitzer in his book *Healing the Culture* outlines four levels of happiness—which for our purposes here I will condense to three:

1. Immediate gratification
2. Ego gratification
3. Looking for the good in others; extending love

Each of those levels is built into us and there is nothing wrong per se with finding happiness at any of them. The problem lies when we seem stuck at one level and believe that happiness can only be achieved there.

In the aftermath of your husband's affair your world probably up-ended. You didn't feel loved and you didn't feel safe. In order to feel better you needed immediate feedback on certain things. Is he still seeing her or not? Does he want the marriage to survive or not? Does he still love me? Where is he right now and what's he doing? Can I afford a divorce? In other words, you were stuck primarily on the first level of happiness.

When you began making comparisons between yourself and "her" your ego was driving you and you were operating from the second level. When one's ego is in play, life becomes a competition—there are winners and losers. If she wins you lose. You worry about your attractiveness or your ability to manage a life being single again. Ego gratification sustains us longer than immediate gratification but eventually we need more ego boosts to continue feeling happy

When you function from the third level of happiness you look beyond yourself. You see a purpose to your life despite hardship. If you are still with your husband you find yourself emphasizing his good qualities rather than focusing on his bad qualities. You don't pretend his bad qualities don't exist or give yourself pats on the back for tolerating them—you simply seek to view him in the fullest light possible, which means recognizing his good qualities.

The problem with levels one and two is that we often require others to function better (or to do our will) in order for us to be happy. We rely on others to compliment us, approve of us, speak well of us, lose to us, or give us what we want in order to feel good. That makes us dependent. At the first two levels our life is squarely in the realm of the material. Only at higher levels do we find happiness beyond the physical realm. For example, at the material level a flower has a shape, size, and fragrance. At a higher level of awareness it can appear to us as beauty or a symbol of love. To a child a tall mountain might simply be enormously large and fun to explore. To an adult it, looking at such a mountain can be inspiring. Children might count stars in the sky and ask how they manage to stay "up there" while an adult might be awestruck by the vastness of the universe and contemplate her immortal soul.

Detach from Outcome

Most people find it hard living with uncertainty when the stakes are high. Will the marriage succeed or fail? They become focused on outcome and cannot relax until they know where they stand. Decades of research that examined why it was that some people coped well during adversity and some didn't concluded the following: people who cope well generally believe that matters will work out as well as can be expected. In other words, they have hope—not that matters will work out the way *they* desire, but that matters will work out for the best regardless. Such people are not merely optimistic; they have *emotionally detached from needing a specific outcome.* They believe that forces are often at work to bring about certain ends—ends that can only be perceived when one is at enough of a distance to gain perspective. (Imagine watching a movie where it looks as if a huge fire is out of control. The camera pans back and suddenly you see that the fire is in a cozy fireplace. You need perspective to really understand what's happened.)

Detaching from outcome happens when you realize that you had very little control over your situation to begin with. You have some degree of influence but not nearly as much power as you think. It means being willing to entertain the possibility that you don't always know what is in your best interest. I counseled a woman whose fiancé broke off their engagement and ended their relationship weeks before her wedding. Devastated at first, one year later she confided, "Not marrying him was the best thing that ever happened to me." She discovered that her fiancé had character traits she never saw before. He also had led a secret life and had been lying to her a great deal. She moved on, lost weight, felt terrific about her appearance, and was grateful things turned out the way they did. *But she didn't have that awareness at the time it first happened.*

By detaching from outcome you move from insisting that you know what's best to a more humble attitude that says "I must trust when things aren't going my way that I am still being served in some fashion." Have you ever experienced a disappointment or loss only to realize—perhaps years later—that there were great benefits to your not getting what you thought you wanted? That is the concept you must hold on to. By doing that you release your ego—your need to be in complete control of your destiny—and allow forces that know better to guide you.

Get Rid of "Should" Statements

As you deal with infidelity your head will fill with "should" statements. For example:

- I should be over this by now.
- This should never have happened.

- He should understand when I don't want to have sex with him.
- He should completely forget about her.
- I should be more trusting by now.
- He shouldn't have put his needs above the marriage.

The list can go on. Byron Katie's wonderful book *Loving What Is* shows readers a simple way to examine their dysfunctional thoughts. One way is to simply ask, "Do I know that's true?" Chances are you have no solid basis for your belief. It is just an opinion you've attached yourself to and now it feels like truth. Is it really true that you should be over this by now? Do you know that it's true that his affair should never have happened? Is it really true that he should completely forget about her?

Once you can doubt these opinions you have more room to breathe. Things don't always play out on your time schedule.

Byron Katie also discusses the "turnaround." This is a technique therapists often use. Simply identify a certain belief, change the pronouns around, and see if the new statement also has validity. For example, "He should completely forget about her" now becomes "I should completely forget about her." Does that second statement make as much a sense as the first? Why do you expect him to forget if you don't? The statement "He should be more at ease with me" now becomes "I should be more at ease with him." Is that true? A third way to examine a belief is to change it to the opposite. So "I hate this" might become "I don't hate this." Could that be true in any way? "This shouldn't have happened" becomes "This should have happened." Can there be any validity at all to that last statement?

Is There a Spiritual Reason for Your Situation?

Do you believe in God? If so, do you believe that sometimes bad things can happen for spiritual reasons? If you do, could there possibly be a spiritual reason for your suffering over an affair? You don't necessarily need to come up with a clear answer. Just by speculating on that possibility it can give you pause and perhaps lower your anxiety and raise your awareness just a bit. Certainly, bad things can result from an affair—the end of a marriage, suffering for the kids, a blow to one's esteem, financial distress. But is it possible that you need to learn certain life lessons in order to become a stronger person? Do you need to learn how to forgive? If so, this is a perfect opportunity. Have you been a doormat and people-pleaser? Maybe you need now to stand up for yourself and not be mistreated. Have you secretly been unhappy in the marriage anyway but had no way out? Maybe now is the opportunity. Do you have a big ego and need to learn humility? Crises can happen so that:

- An overly judgmental person may learn tolerance.
- An impatient person learns to trust and have faith.
- A selfish person learns to give.
- A giving person learns to meet her own needs, too.
- A perfectionist learns to accept imperfection.
- A bitter person learns forgiveness.
- A guilt-ridden person finds redemption.
- An insecure person learns she has worth and capabilities.
- An "I'll do it myself" person learns interdependence.

- An "I can't do it myself" person learns self-reliance.
- A materialist learns that the physical realm passes away.

Even if you doubt there are spiritual reasons for your suffering, ask yourself this question: if there were spiritual reasons, what might they be? What have been—or could be—the possible benefits to you for having to endure a betrayal? The Sunday after 9/11 churches in America were filled to capacity. Obviously that isn't the case today but for a while people realized they needed something more than themselves to believe in. Getting in greater touch with the spiritual side of life can be of great benefit. However, it often takes adversity for people to do that.

Seven Healing Beliefs

It's easy to feel forsaken after a deep loss or betrayal. It can be a struggle to get up in the morning. But as you have (hopefully) seen from this book, how you think about a situation affects how you feel more than the actual situation does. Attitude often becomes destiny.

The following are seven beliefs that, if embraced fully, will lead to emotional and spiritual healing. When you look at a problem in a new way it often appears less of a problem.

Healing Belief #1: All Problems Are Temporary

It's true. No problem lasts forever. Yes, a situation might always remain (a permanent loss or injury, for example) but the negative effects of that situation will change. You will adapt and grow. If your marriage survives and thrives, then years from now when you recall this period of your life it will not carry the heavy emotional weight it now does. If you move on from the marriage and begin a new life, the anxieties and fears you first face will one day subside. The level of pain you now feel will change. Contrast this attitude with the belief "I fear that I'll always feel the way I do now." But does that make sense in light of your experiences in life? Haven't you felt loss or disappointment—saying goodbye to friends, relocating, failing to get the promotion—only to somehow move past those feelings? Perhaps you still dearly miss a loved one who has died. But over time your grief changes. You smile more at the loved one's memory and cry less. In the midst of depression it seems the pain will never end. But that is not the way of things. Everything in life changes. Everything moves on.

Healing Belief #2: The People Who Hurt Me Don't Do So Because I Am Unlovable

Let your motto be "Don't take it personally, even when it's personal." I'm sure you've blamed yourself in some ways for your husband's infidelity. "If only I'd done this . . . maybe he wouldn't have done that . . ." And true, you have faults. You are weak in ways and so is he. The choices he made to deal with his unhappiness say much about him and not so much about you. You made different choices. The fact that he may no longer be in love with you, or that his love for you wasn't strong enough for him to avoid an affair, says nothing about your lovability or worth. The affair doesn't define you. To think otherwise is to make him the final authority of how lovable you are. Is he really that highly advanced and emotionally mature as to be able to determine without question your lovability? I didn't think so. Who made him God?

If you believe you are not lovable because of his affair, then it touched on some older hurts from your past. You simply have a store-house of accumulated wounds and a faulty belief system attached to those wounds. What if you believed "I am worthwhile and lovable despite what happened?" How would you act if you believed such a thought? You'd act with more optimism, self-esteem, and integrity. (Self-esteem isn't something you have as much as it's something you do. Act with self-esteem.)

Healing Belief #3: My Life Can Still Be Meaningful

Suffering is bad enough. But when our suffering means something (such as when we make sacrifices for our children's sake) then suffering does not lead to despair. The meanest form of suffering is suffering with no meaning. It's helpful to realize that in spite of your suffering—and even *because* of your suffering—your life can be more meaningful than you ever thought possible. You must be open to the possibility that life has more to offer you and that you have more to offer life. How do we find meaning? Viktor Frankl, in his classic book *Man's Search for Meaning*, said that we find meaning through loving relationships, creative work, and the way we respond to adversity. If we respond to adversity with determination and hope, we will likely change ourselves for the better.

Many people have a reason to get up in the morning until one day their life changes. Maybe they suffer a severe illness, or a spouse dies, or the children finally leave home and are independent. Now the reasons they once had for pushing on in life have changed. For a while they may feel their life has no meaning. Sometimes life hands you a meaning (such as when you have children who now depend on you). But often we have to make life meaningful when we're not sure how. It might be that others still depend upon you. Or perhaps you wish to learn new skills. Ironically, even the search to find meaning can itself become meaningful as you learn more about yourself in the process.

Healing Belief #4: I Can Get Through This

People who cope during trying times believe they will eventually land on their feet. They may not know precisely how or when but they know they'll get there. It isn't enough to be persistent. Persistence takes you only so far until you become exhausted or lose faith if matters aren't working out the way you'd hoped. You need determination, which involves persistence plus purpose. You have to find a purpose to keep going, a reason to get to the other side.

Determination is aided by patience. Patience isn't simply gritting your teeth and tolerating the wait. Patience comes from knowing that you are on the right track. If you know that, you can tolerate the wait. If you don't know if you're on the right track you will become impatient quickly and need to find out where you stand.

Will he or won't he stay with you? Do you or don't you want him back? Will the marriage ever be better? It's an illusion that you need to know those answers right now. You can have hope, or you can be confused about what you want. But those answers will play out in time if you don't have them already. Patience comes from trusting that what's happening now—whatever the reality of the day is—is part of the process. If you want the marriage to work and he isn't so sure, you have two options: be highly anxious until the answer is clear or trust that this is the best that things can be for now. You can't force him to want you. If nothing happens as time goes on, you may have to make a choice you'd rather not make. But the alternative is to remain steadfast to a relationship he can't commit to—how can that make you happy?

How do you know if you're on the right track? That's not easy to determine. Do you know for sure that if you get what you want you'll really be happy? Do you know for sure that if you don't get what you want you'll really be unhappy? You're probably on the right track if you have clear goals and are making strides to meet those goals *and* you possess a humble philosophy that says you're open to being guided elsewhere just in case your goals are not in your best interest. In other words, when rafting in white-water rapids it's necessary sometimes to stop trying to steer. You have a direction and a goal but you must also allow other forces to propel you forward at times.

Healing Belief #5: I Am Grateful

I'm aware as I write these words that you may be in the midst of feeling very hurt, very bitter, or very scared. And suggesting that you cheer up and focus on the things in life you're grateful for sounds awfully insensitive.

It's okay to be ungrateful right now, if that's how you feel. You're certainly not grateful for his affair. Any time anyone tries to tell you that you shouldn't feel the way you are feeling (and you are in deep pain), that person doesn't understand you and you are lonelier for it.

Perhaps it is only when we feel understood and allowed to have feelings of anger, rage, guilt, or fear that we can begin to let go of our grip on them at least somewhat. When we don't feel understood we often hold on to our pain, hoping that others might start to pay closer attention and understand us better. Once you feel understood, you can open your mind to other possibilities. Gratitude is one of them. You might think, "Of course I'm grateful for my children . . . my friends . . . my lifestyle . . . but those things aren't the issue right now." Those things are part of you and therefore *are* the issue as well. When you look for truth about your situation don't fail to see the truths of your life that can be easily overlooked during times of trouble. Those can be precisely the things that can help sustain you.

Gratitude must not be a passing thought but a persistent theme. Do you have your health? Do you have children you love? Friends who care? Then despite what your husband did you also have much to be grateful for. It's okay to feel grateful and ungrateful at the same time. If you're angry that life has dealt you an unfair blow and that you didn't deserve to be betrayed, you can at the same time be grateful for what you have been given. Don't try to let one side of your feelings win out over the other side. Let them coexist since both are true for you at the moment. "I accept that life has been unfair to me and I accept that life has been generous to me."

Gratitude is not meant to cover up pain or to pretend you haven't suffered a loss. Gratitude is meant to reveal that there is more to your life that is good than you may be able to consider at the moment.

Healing Belief #6: There Is a Future for Me

It isn't enough to know you can get through it somehow. What's on the other side once you get there? Will you have a future that's worth having? You may be unable to answer that now. If you're scared about realistic possibilities such as loss of income or loss of child custody—let alone loss of the marriage—or if you're scared that your marriage might "work out" but be held together by string, your future may not seem bright.

When we function at our lower levels of coping we push aside things like hope and trust and instead need something more tangible. We want to know for sure. We want answers, not wishful thinking. But at more advanced levels of coping we realize that outcomes are rarely in our control. We can control only our part of the process and even then we do so imperfectly. Coping at higher levels involves letting go, not clutching. It involves accepting the reality that outcomes often unfold in their own way and in their own time despite our efforts. Our efforts can go only so far before we must give way to forces outside our power. Coping, then, requires the nurturing of hope—hope that a future does exist that will be worthwhile and meaningful.

There are four underpinnings to hope.

1. **The felt sense of being understood.** You need to know that your feelings make sense to at least one other person, that you're not crazy or hysterical. When you feel understood you don't feel so alone or without options. Once understood, hope takes root.

2. **Faith that you have resources to cope.** You may possess inner strengths you can call upon or you may ask for others to help you along the way. You may rely on your family, friends, clergy, or a therapist to help hold you up along the way. These are the people who will be there for you when you get to the other side of your adversity.

3. **Committed work.** You can't simply wish for a future. You must do all that you can to create a life that will work for you. When you are plugging away you haven't lost hope.

4. **Meaningfulness.** As stated earlier, once you believe that your life will have meaning no matter what happens then you'll believe that a future waits for you. By believing you have a future you are claiming that the hurt will not hold you back.

Healing Belief #7: My Life Will Make a Difference to Someone I Haven't Met Yet

A man I knew was grieving the death of his spouse and felt he had little to live for. One day while he was standing at a busy intersection waiting to cross, a young boy near him ran out into traffic. The man grabbed the boy, who was inches away from being struck and certainly severely injured if not killed. Later he spoke to me about how his life, meaningless when he awoke that fateful day, had become suddenly meaningful. He'd made a difference in someone's life. He imagined that young boy growing up, having children, perhaps involved with a career that helps others, and realized his one act had profound consequences. That experience opened his eyes to the possibility that his life could be important for other people as well.

You don't know what awaits you, but the more involved with life you are the more likely you are to have a positive impact on someone. Such an attitude can keep you moving forward with the realization that while your marriage is important, your life is more than your marriage.

trusting your gut: increasing faith in him and yourself

After an affair, the assumptions you made about yourself, your marriage, and your husband now seem like broken shards of glass. You used to think you were desirable and worthwhile; now you feel replaceable. You used to think the marriage was sturdy—held together by devotion and love; now it seems fragile and a sham. You once saw him as trustworthy and loving—someone who'd give his life for you and never purposely hurt you deeply; now you view him as two-faced, a liar, and a manipulator, and you wonder if you really know him at all. Those assumptions are the floorboards of your life. Now you're walking on something unsturdy, something that feels as if it could give way at any moment and send you sprawling.

If your marriage survives and thrives, trust will be the last thing that falls into place. It simply takes time. You may feel more loving, more sexual, and more affectionate—and trust will grow—but you'll reach a point of perhaps a 90 percent level of trust and find it slow going to progress any further. One woman explained it this way: "When I went on a diet and lost a lot of weight, the final ten pounds were the hardest to take off. After my husband had an affair, I came close to my goal of trusting him completely again but it took a long time to reach the finish line."

The Ingredients of Trust

Obviously, trust-building will have a lot to do with how your partner acts from now on. Unless he devotes himself to your relationship and tries to win you back, there will be very little trust. But it isn't enough that he act trustworthy. You must *believe* and *feel* that he *is* trustworthy. That means that regaining trust will actually have as much to do with you—your thoughts, feelings, and actions—as with him. He must act in ways that show he is accountable for his decision to have an affair by being willing to restrict his activities and reassure you of his faithfulness. And you must be willing to take small leaps of faith—over and over—where you risk being hurt again. Trust requires a willingness to believe when there are reasons to disbelieve, a willingness to have faith in him when you don't know with absolute certainty that your faith is justified. (You may think that isn't possible. However, driving a car requires trust that you will arrive at your destination safely even though a possibility exists you won't.) There are four major steps to take when trying to rebuild trust. Those steps are like rows of bricks that gradually create a solid wall of trust. The four steps are:

1. He takes accountability for his actions and restructures his life.
2. You modify your vigilance of him over time.
3. You re-examine your assessment of him.
4. You re-examine your assessment of yourself.

But bricks are held in place by mortar. Here the mortar is made of the small, everyday things you and he do that can add to and strengthen the sturdiness of your trust. For example, thoughtful gestures, doing enjoyable things together, small shows of affection or tenderness, and caring conversations all hold the bricks in place.

Accountability

He must admit that what he did was wrong and be willing to restrict his activities in ways that will offer you reassurances that he's not still cheating. And he must convey by his attitude that he cares deeply that you've been hurt. A man who falls short in these areas will espouse a "Get over it" philosophy that shows insensitivity to your pain. He will resist any restrictions on his life ("Why should I have to come right home after work?") and make you feel at fault for mistrusting him ("I told you I wouldn't cheat on you again. It's your problem if you won't believe me!"). Such a man has a huge ego, may still be involved with the other woman, and cannot be trusted. However, if your spouse expresses at least some desire to heal the marriage (remember, he may be uncertain what he wants; he may still have feelings for her), then at a minimum he must be willing to restructure his daily life and be willing to be "checked up on" by you if you are to regain any trust in him.

To restructure his life he must curtail outside activities that you consider "risky." That may include office parties, some business trips (it may not be possible to keep his job and eliminate all trips), hanging out with friends after work, and certain hobbies where he might have opportunities to flirt or cheat. For example, if he met his girlfriend at the gym, you might insist he work out at home. He also must allow you access to his cell phone, e-mails, laptop, checkbook, credit card statements, bank accounts, or anything else you might deem necessary (rummaging through his car or wallet) in order for you to feel more reassured that he is not in contact with her or hiding pertinent information. If he tends to stay up later than you and go on the computer, you might require that he only get on the computer when you're awake. You might decide to purchase some software that keeps track of all computer activities. (None of this is done to punish him. These are *temporary* measures designed to help you ease some of your anxiety.)

If he used to meet his girlfriend at a certain time during the day (right before work, during lunch, right after work) he might instead call you at those times, or have you call him. The two of you might meet for lunch or agree to do something pleasant together immediately after work—exercise, go for a walk, prepare a meal, play with the kids, and so forth.

It's also essential that he not get impatient with your many questions. As discussed in a previous chapter, questions about the details of the affair—who, when, where, why—are best handled during a regularly *scheduled* discussion. Still, innocent questions like "What did you do today?" or "Why didn't you pick up when I called?" will feel to him like the inquisition. The more willingly he responds to those questions straightforwardly and without "attitude," the more comfortable you will feel.

If the other woman was more than just a one-night stand—and especially if she had feelings for him—it's almost guaranteed she will try to contact him again (and again) even if he told her, "It's over between us." And if he has feelings for her he will almost certainly be in contact with her even if he promised you he wouldn't. This is a treacherous area for you both. He needs to understand that any contact with her—even if you never find out about it—will halt any progress in the marriage and turn his affections away from you and toward her—even just a little. There can be no pretending about this. Movement toward the other woman, even in small, seemingly innocent ways ("I just met her for coffee to find out how she was doing . . . I just called her to find out how her son's operation went") is movement away from the marriage. It will stir his passions for her, and even if you never find out about it he has yet another secret.

However, even that situation can be eased if he promises to inform you about every meeting or call. Ideally, he will bite the bullet and steer clear of her. But she will inevitably contact him. He then needs to tell you about it. If she left him a phone message he should let you hear it and not return the call unless you and he decide together that he can. (If he tells you she left a message but he deletes it without letting you hear it, that will only raise your suspicions.) If there is a good probability that you and he might run into her (she lives nearby, they work together, or you share similar friends and social connections) it's best to have a plan on how you two will handle it. (It is *never* a good idea to insist he make derisive comments to her or otherwise embarrass her in public—nor should you. That will inflame the situation—perhaps make her want to recontact him just to annoy you—and may make him be furious with you. Do nothing that will make him feel sorry for her.) Ideally, you two would act in a manner that shows you are back together even if your marriage is still quite strained. You might, for example, hold hands in her presence, or hold each other more closely. Ignoring her completely is the best option.

Modifying Your Vigilance

Checking up on him, going through his personal belongings, and hiring a private investigator can help alleviate uncertainty. Such actions are like painkillers. They ease your pain in the short term but can become addictive over time. In order to rebuild trust you must be willing to cut back your need for such things and engage in them less often. There is no time frame. On average, the betrayed spouse keeps him on a tight leash for two or three months at least before easing up. But that can vary depending upon your unique circumstances. The less cooperative he is, the longer you will remain vigilant and mistrusting.

In some ways you will become a probation officer. It's not a fun job, since while the two of you are trying to feel like a couple you must act in ways that make you his overseer or boss. He may start to feel like a teenager being constrained by an overly strict parent. But even probation officers eventually abandon continuous vigilance and give random tests. You might, for example, not call him every day at lunch hour but only every so often. You won't ask him detailed questions about his day quite so often. This can add to your anxiety and uncertainty initially but it can add to your confidence in him over time.

Avoid asking him questions that will only make you heartsick or doubt his honesty. Avoid questions like "Did you think of her at all today? Do you ever smile when you think about her? Do you think of her while making love to me? Was your affair worth it?"

Also avoid questions that are really jabs in disguise. "Do you ever stop to think about the harm you did to this family? How can you say you love your children if you were willing to uproot their lives for her? How can you ever set foot in church again? How can I ever hear you say you love me and believe you? How can you look yourself in the mirror every day? What makes you think you have the right to call yourself a decent man or a good father?"

You can ease up on your vigilance of him by coming up with a list of positive things he can do that would make you believe he does care about you and the marriage. For example, you might ask him to:

- Spend some enjoyable time with you within thirty minutes of getting home.
- Go on more dates with you.
- Plan a date to renew your wedding vows.
- Find one enjoyable activity or hobby you can do together (attend a workshop on how to give great massages; learn to dance; join a choir; create a garden; attend interesting workshops or classes).
- Make sure you have twenty minutes a day (on hectic days) of quality couple time.

If you are worried about your financial situation should the marriage break up, you might also insist that some monies be put aside for you so you have cash available "just in case." If you can breathe a sigh of relief that funds are available should you need them, you may be able to relinquish some of your control over his day-to-day activities as you try to trust him more.

Be Prepared for Unexpected Sadness

As you ease up on overseeing every aspect of his life you'd expect to feel some relief, perhaps a bit of joy that you are starting to regain trust. And that may happen. But mistrust is fed by anxiety and anger. As those two emotions lessen over time, you may discover that you still have some grief that was pushed aside somewhat by worry and bitterness. Since you are less hyperactive and less preoccupied with wondering if he can be trusted, you may have more time to feel sad over all that's happened. You may feel more grief at the loss of innocence in your marriage, exhausted by the energy drain, and sad at the realization that you are helpless to stop an affair if he truly wants to have one.

Such feelings indicate that you have entered more into the sub-dued phase of coping. He's displaying more trustworthiness, you're working on rebuilding the marriage, the other woman may be finally out of the way—but you're not happy. It's like waking up on Christmas morning with your family, presents everywhere, but someone you love isn't there and you can't find a way to feel as happy as you'd like. That someone—now as you try to heal the marriage—is yourself. You're there but you're not there. A spark has gone out of you. So to keep adding to your trust and sense of faith that the future can still be bright, you must take a closer look at how you think.

Re-Examine Your Assessment of Him

It's not fair to label someone as either trustworthy or untrustworthy. The better question is: Under what conditions is a person likely to be trustworthy and under what conditions is he less likely to be trust-worthy? Framing it that way allows you to see his positive traits while at the same time accepting that he has weaknesses, too. For example, you may have a close friend whom you consider trustworthy. She's there for you at two in the morning if you need her; she will drop everything to help you in a crisis—but maybe she gossips a little about you behind your back. Is she trustworthy? To a large extent, yes. But she has her flaws, as well. Many "honest" people will still sneak out of work early some days, "borrow" items from their workplace, dent someone's car but not leave a note, or tell the officer, "The light was still green!" when they know they went through a red light.

When you ask yourself, "Is my guy trustworthy?" you are asking three things. You want to measure his trustworthiness in all three areas.

1. Is he reliable?
2. Does he tell the truth?
3. Is he faithful?

Reliability

To begin having more faith in him, first ask if he's reliable. Does he bring home his paycheck or does he gamble it away or spend it recklessly? Does he perform his role as father? Can you count on him to take care of things that he's responsible for? If you were ill could you count on him to step up to the plate and do what needs doing? If you needed emotional support for some concern (a parent dies or is ill, problems at work, and so on) would he be there for you? Does he show up to work on time, pay his bills, call his parents, or do any of the other ordinary things that an outside observer would say indicated reliability? If so, give him credit for that.

Truthfulness

Does he tell the truth? Obviously he got a failing grade recently in that area. But you must look at the big picture. Does he usually keep his promises? Remember, lying about an affair—which is often more difficult to deal with than any sexual indiscretion—is what happens when people cheat. Rarely do people cheat and come home and spill the beans. (In fact, if an affair has ended and an unsuspecting spouse had no clue, it can do more harm than good to confess the affair. Honesty isn't always the best policy.) If he lied because he fully intended to see this other woman (while denying that he was) and he was simply biding his time and manipulating you until he left you for her, then his lying was despicable. But you have bigger problems—he has no interest in staying married. If his affair was unplanned on his part and he still has feelings for you and a desire to see if the marriage can be salvaged, and you confronted him with suspicious evidence, his lying about the affair is a problem but a more understandable one. It wasn't done to take advantage of you but, in his mind anyway, to keep the situation from getting worse. Of course deceit is almost always revealed over time and instead of preventing things from getting worse it causes things to be ten times worse. Still, his deceitfulness may not represent an overall character trait but more so a character weakness that shows up under certain conditions. Weaknesses can be strengthened.

At this point, measure his truthfulness by asking yourself, "Did he seem to be truthful *today?*" If yes, score one for the marriage.

Faithfulness

You can never be absolutely sure he is faithful. (Nor can he be absolutely sure you are faithful.) The best you can do for now is ask yourself if all the evidence points to his being faithful today (this week, this month). If weeks pass and you keep answering in the affirmative, you can begin to change your opinion of him as someone who is more trustworthy in that area than he once had been.

Re-Examine Your Assessment of Yourself

Remaining mistrustful is a form of anxiety management. You're anxious and worried he may cheat on you again or lie to you so you remain mistrustful and hypervigilant. This helps keep your anxiety from skyrocketing. But as I said before, you can become addicted to being mistrustful. As you try to show more trust and make yourself more vulnerable to being hurt, your anxiety will rise (similar to having withdrawal symptoms from a drug). If that scares you or makes you too uncomfortable, you will revert to being more mistrusting and more "on alert," which will temporarily ease your heightened anxiety—much like a pain pill eases the throbbing.

To break the addiction you must be willing to suffer anxiety until it eases on its own. If you can't do that, if you keep holding on to your mistrust, there are probably four reasons why:

1. You don't feel safe.
2. You wish to retaliate.
3. You wish to avoid being made a fool of (again).
4. You doubt your worthwhileness.

Let's examine those more closely.

You Don't Feel Safe

Here you decide to maintain control (although control is an illusion—you have less control than you think) over your situation by maintaining strict rules and always doubting he can ever be trusted. To be more trusting and to ease up on the rules makes you feel too vulnerable. But as any prison guard will tell you, prisoners find ways to bend strict rules. The longer you remain mistrustful, the more unhappy and despairing your husband will be. If he shows signs of giving up on the marriage it will only reinforce your belief that he wants to be with someone else and you will probably become harsher in your control.

Feeling safe comes about only by relinquishing control and allowing the chips to fall where they may. You must allow him to demonstrate his trustworthiness by giving him more freedoms.

You Wish to Retaliate

You might be holding on to a mistrusting attitude as a way to punish him. So you check through his things or insist he not go out with his buddies after work not just to alleviate your anxiety but to "stick it to him." The desire to punish is understandable. Eventually he'll catch on and resent what you're doing. You might think "So what?" but you're giving him a reason to deflect guilt off of himself and put it on to you. Now *you're* the difficult one. *You're* the one undermining progress.

You Wish to Avoid Looking Like a Fool

If you want your marriage to work and you want to regain trust you have to risk that he'll cheat on you again and you'll feel like a fool—again. Staying on high alert and refusing to trust him any farther than you can throw him will ultimately result in the demise of your happiness and probably your relationship. Yes, some people have a "Throw the bum out!" mentality and would consider you foolish for giving him another chance. But giving another chance might well be a noble thing. If you're doing it because you took your vows seriously, or because you have children, or because you still love him, or because he seems to sincerely want a second chance, those are noble reasons.

If you give him a second chance and he betrays that trust, he will look like the bigger fool. Not you.

You Doubt Your Worthwhileness

You may be holding on to mistrust because you can't risk losing him. And you can't risk losing him because you doubt you're worthwhile enough for anybody else. No doubt, a cheating spouse can take a large chunk out of anybody's self-esteem. But if you've carried a deeper sense of inadequacy for a longer time, you have more work to do. (Building your esteem is beyond the scope of this book.) Keep in mind that if you think he stays with you because you have him on a short leash, you will never get what you really want. You want to know that he is with you out of choice, not because he's handcuffed. You must be willing to turn him loose. If he still wants to be with you then you can trust he is doing so out of his own choice.

Time brings perspective. At first, many betrayed wives think, "I can't believe he did this *to me.*" Over time, that changes to "I can't believe he did this." That is ultimately followed by "I don't like that he did it but I must accept it." Those are important differences. It's understandable to take an affair very personally. But many people can understand why others may have affairs *in general*—when it isn't personal—but cannot accept it when it's done to them. It's hard to detach yourself from your situation, but try to imagine that your husband was someone you didn't know and you learned he'd had an affair. You probably wouldn't think, "I can't believe he did that!" You'd probably think he must have had his reasons.

Asking "How could he do this *to me!*" misses the larger picture. He did do it and he did it for a number of reasons (not necessarily good ones). As long as you make an emphasis on *"to me"* you will have a harder time listening to him and understanding him. You will feel more vulnerable and less trusting.

construction work: strengthening the foundation of the relationship

The way couples handle the aftermath of an affair is similar to the way a physician might respond to a patient suffering a heart attack: any other medical problems that existed before the crisis take a back seat to the immediate concerns. A physician may take note that the patient has high cholesterol and is prediabetic, but responding to the heart attack comes first. Similarly, any relationship problems that existed prior to the affair seem to pale in comparison to the impact of the infidelity.

It's a juggling act. But at some point the tide turns and the relationship must be examined as a whole while the affair becomes secondary. Perhaps there were relationship problems that contributed to his choice to have an affair. Or maybe there were no relationship problems but steps must now be taken to strengthen the relationship so as to avoid a future betrayal.

Identifying Triggers to Future Infidelity

It is hard to rebuild a relationship after an affair if there is good reason to think it might happen again. No relationship is affair-proof, despite what die-hard romantics might wish to believe. I've worked with countless individuals who've cheated and who never would have predicted they'd have done such a thing. But steps can be taken to greatly improve the odds that it won't happen again.

Risk factors to an affair can be due to relationship problems, individual issues, and current situational factors. Often it is a combination of those factors.

Major relationship issues that increase the risk of infidelity are:

- Low level of intimacy and closeness
- Diminished goodwill
- Poor ability to handle conflict

Major personal factors include:

- Difficulty making a commitment; fears of intimacy; difficulty trusting
- A preference for pleasure, immediate gratification, and a need for regular ego-boosts that take precedence over the values of loyalty and self-sacrifice
- Sexual addiction

Major situational factors include:

- The death of a loved one and other life stressors or transitions (midlife concerns, becoming a parent, kids leaving home)
- A lifestyle conducive to flirting, partying, and philandering
- Jobs that put one in intimate contact with others for extended periods

As stated earlier in this book, the individual/personal factors are key. That's because all of the other risk factors get funneled through the individual and his overall level of psychological maturity, insight, and coping skills. (For example, a healthy, insightful adult more quickly discerns whether a marital problem is based upon some former childhood injury or loss.) Someone who has strong values about faithfulness but who is less adept at managing stress or who needs strong ego-boosts to a flagging self-esteem may succumb to an affair, whereas someone with an ability to manage conflict well may not. (That may help to explain why more men who report they have a "happy" marriage still cheat.) Someone who has become emotionally distant from a spouse is more vulnerable to cheating than if the couple has a rewarding level of intimacy and closeness.

If you're the betrayed spouse, you have less influence over the personal factors affecting your partner. True, if his self-esteem is low there may be ways for you to show him appreciation or make him feel important. However, self-esteem problems usually go deeper and he will need to make headway on that issue himself—perhaps with the help of a therapist. But you can do something about the relationship factors that might be operating. Anything you can do to help strengthen overall intimacy and improve the way the two of you deal with conflict, anger, and the inevitable differences that arise in any long-term relationship will reduce the odds that either one of you will stray.

What Is Genuine Intimacy?

When people hear the word "intimacy" they usually think it has to do with relating sexually or having a deep personal conversation. But intimacy is much broader and more important than that. You can have a very intimate moment where no words are spoken and there is no sexual contact. *Intimacy is the closeness that develops when a couple mutually reveals more of who they are to each other in an atmosphere of safety and acceptance.* There are three key ingredients to that definition:

1. Intimacy is *mutual*. It cannot be one-sided.
2. Intimacy involves self-revelation. So someone who is private, closed-off, suspicious, manipulative, or fearful of self-disclosure will automatically limit the level of intimacy that is possible.
3. Intimacy must happen in an atmosphere of safety and acceptance. Hostility, ridicule, dismissing another's feelings or concerns, rejection, intimidation, and anything that makes one feel less than safe or acceptable will limit intimacy.

It can be discouraging for a member of a couple to try to be more open and take risks by saying what's on his or her mind, only to be met with an indignant "How can you think such a thing!" It's common for one to complain that the other doesn't talk enough, while the nontalker complains, "When I do speak up, all I get is flak." That's why the SAIL method of communication discussed in Chapter 7 includes "acceptance" of what the other says as an important part of effective dialogue.

Intimacy is magical because when a couple experiences it at its deepest, fullest level, they can make many relationship mistakes and still feel connected and close. That's because true intimacy is accompanied by a great deal of goodwill. And goodwill allows mistakes to be made without it being much of a problem. Contrast that with couples who don't have enough goodwill. As soon as someone says the wrong thing, even if he or she claims, "That's not what I meant!" it can be too late and an argument might follow.

Intimacy is not reserved for your primary relationship only. You can have close, intimate friends, for example. However, in a marriage or other committed (and romantic) relationship, intimacy involves a sexual component that is (supposedly) not part of other intimate relationships. That is one reason why a sexual affair can be so painful for the betrayed spouse. Not only does it raise fears about the future of the relationship, the uniqueness of the intimate relationship (sexual expression, pillow-talk, and so forth) has been diluted.

The Four Pathways to Intimacy

Through my experience counseling couples, I have developed a theory that couples can achieve lasting intimacy through four pathways. Also known as "The Four T's," they are:

1. Intimacy through *Thought*
2. Intimacy through *Talk*
3. Intimacy through *Touch*
4. Intimacy through *Togetherness*

Your levels of intimacy in all areas can range from none to high. Since you are in the midst of coping with an affair your overall levels of intimacy will be weaker than usual. But what were they like in the months or years before the affair? Chances are that one or more of the four pathways was weaker than it should have been. Now it's important to strengthen all four areas as much as possible if your relationship is to heal.

Intimacy Through Thought

You can generate more intimacy without moving a muscle. How? By the way you think about your partner. If you don't make room in your mind for positive, warm thoughts about your mate, you'll be less likely to make room for him in your daily schedule. How do you talk to yourself about him? (And what does he say to himself about you?) How often do you think about him?

Couples have basically three ways of relating to each other: they approach each other (move toward greater intimacy), avoid each other (move away from intimacy), or argue (struggle with intimacy). All three operate within a relationship but one style tends to predominate. It's the same with how you think. Your thoughts about your partner during an average day will make you feel closer to him, make you move away from him, or make you want to clash with him. When it comes to rebuilding intimacy after an affair, you want to minimize the latter two.

The Approach Thinker

If this is your predominant mode, you tend to be friendly and outgoing and express emotions more readily. You may be uneasy with conflict. That has its benefits and drawbacks. You may wish to "make nice" quickly to avoid conflict but on the other hand you will be more likely to find ways to resolve problems rather than sit and stew over them.

As an approach thinker you tend to be optimistic. Thoughts about your partner are more often positive, exciting, and oriented around connecting. You'll be more likely to give the benefit of the doubt.

Approach thinkers sometimes come across as very needy and feel threatened by distance—even when some degree of emotional space is healthy in a relationship. However, unresolved childhood issues or some other emotional traumas, losses, or rejections can cause an "approach person" to hook up with someone who is more distant or afraid of too much closeness. In that case, the approach person's desire for closeness is based on fulfilling an unmet need from childhood. Often, unmet needs lead to someone choosing a partner who will repeat—to some extent—unresolved childhood issues. Thus, a woman who craved more attention and affection as a child may hook up with a man who offers affection somewhat sparingly and who easily feels smothered. However, a woman who received a great deal of healthy love and affection as a child and who desires closeness and intimacy with a partner is more likely to find a man who has a similar desire for intimacy.

The Avoidance Thinker

If you are this type, you hate conflict and withdraw quickly when conversations get tense. You tend to keep a blind eye to situations, minimize any problems, and only take action when matters have gotten way out of hand. On the surface you seem relaxed and easy-going. That may be true to an extent. But much of the calmness is due to a driving desire to not make waves or act emotionally.

Do You Have Enough Relationship Goodwill?

It's not enough to say you love your partner. Goodwill develops when partners regularly send a message that conveys *I love being around you, I admire you, I look forward to our time together, I'd go out of my way for you, I have fun with you, you excite me, I miss you when you're not here.* You can cultivate goodwill by thinking positive and exciting thoughts about your mate.

More men than women tend to act and think this way. Men shut down more from conflict and are less likely to keep finding ways to increase closeness in a relationship (once it has become well established and comfortable) than are women. On the plus side, avoidance thinkers can be a calm in the center of a storm and not likely to stir up conflict unnecessarily. On the down side, they want disagreements to simply be over and done with and may make concessions that are unrealistic ("Fine, fine, whatever you say").

Avoidance thinkers are more accepting of lower levels of intimacy. They are like washing machines—sturdy, reliable, can do their job for many years—but be somewhat boring or unimaginative. If an avoidance-type man is hooked up with an approach-type woman there will be occasional dissatisfaction on both sides. But deep down he *needs* his partner to seek closeness since he does want it. But he also fears having too much of it.

An avoidance thinker is less likely to think about his or her partner during the day except for practical reasons. For them, it's "out of sight, out of mind." When trying to rebuild after an affair, this type of thinker must try to think much more of the partner, especially in ways that increase fondness, attraction, and connectedness.

The Argumentative Thinker

This person tends to be competitive, likes to be right, has a hard time admitting mistakes, and tends to impulsively blame others when things go wrong. This person may easily confront others—or just the opposite. He or she may rarely speak up about resentments but stew repeatedly over the unfairness in a relationship. While avoidance thinkers may not think about a problem once having left the house and gone to work, argumentative thinkers will build a case in their mind about how their partner was wrong or unfair and become even more angry.

Such a style of thinking sets up a scenario where a small misunderstanding or slight can lead to an immediate rush of anger—because the anger has been simmering underneath all along.

Argumentative thinkers need to value *understanding* their partner more than winning and being right. They have to think less about how others impact them and more about how they are impacting others. They need to care more about mutual give and take and respectful tones than feeling entitled to their anger. When trying to rebuild after an affair, argumentative thinkers should focus on qualities of their spouse they are grateful for and would miss if the spouse were no longer there.

Giving the Benefit of the Doubt

When trust has been destroyed after an affair it can be hard to give a spouse the benefit of the doubt about anything. But in the rebuilding phase, that needs to start happening more. Obviously, if your partner acts in ways that are clearly insensitive or he continues to lie, it's not possible to give him the benefit of the doubt. But if his aim has been to reconcile with you, there comes a point when you must judge his intentions as good even when you dislike something he did. Giving the benefit of the doubt doesn't mean you must overlook things he does that bother you. It means you won't assume the worst about his intentions or motives. So on any given day maybe he forgets something he promised he'd do. Or he seems aloof and preoccupied. Or he's irritable. Yes, inquire what's up. But handle it the way you might if your best female friend had done the same thing rather than automatically judging him harshly.

Intimacy Through Talk

Couples do a lot of talking when trying to reconcile after an affair. But what happens after they've turned a corner, made progress, and the relationship looks as if it will survive? Do intimate conversations continue? Not always. Often there is a reduction in conversation in part because the immediate crisis is over. But partners may avoid intimate discussions for fear of bringing up a sore topic or touching a nerve.

Take the following quiz to see how easy (or not) self-disclosure is for you. Then repeat the quiz by answering the way you think your partner might respond.

1. I express my emotions fairly easily.

   Often _____ Sometimes _____ Rarely _____

2. If something really bothers me I'm likely to mention it.

   Often _____ Sometimes _____ Rarely _____

3. If my spouse is upset I want to hear more about it.

   Often _____ Sometimes _____ Rarely _____

4. If I get teary-eyed I prefer to hide it.

   Often _____ Sometimes _____ Rarely _____

5. It's easier for me to express annoyance or frustration than praise or gratitude.

   Often _____ Sometimes _____ Rarely _____

6. When I'm busy I'd rather not hear anyone else's problems.

Often _____ Sometimes _____ Rarely _____

7. I can admit it when I'm wrong.

Often _____ Sometimes _____ Rarely _____

8. I've been told I'm quick to criticize.

Often _____ Sometimes _____ Rarely _____

The more you checked "Often" in statements 1, 2, 3, and 7, the better you are at enhancing intimacy through conversation. If you answered "Often" to numbers 4, 5, 6, and 8, you will likely withdraw from uncomfortable conversations or be difficult to converse with. "Sometimes" is acceptable as a response but may indicate areas where you need to make some improvements.

As an immediate goal, aim to have about 15 to 20 minutes a day of uninterrupted time together. You don't have to talk that entire time but it needs to feel comfortable and easy while you're together. Chitchatting about your day while giving a shoulder rub or sitting on the back porch to talk about run-of-the-mill topics can be a nice way to make humdrum conversations more cozy and special.

Pay Attention to Hidden Anger, Guilt, or Worry

Conversations quickly get confusing when the surface discussion doesn't deal with any underlying emotional conflicts that are present but unstated. For example, a year after the affair you might think you are not entitled to still feel moments of anger or mistrust. But your partner may pick up on the fact that "something" seems to be bothering you. Or he may have guilt feelings about his cheating and not feel entitled to voice a small complaint about something you did. You might detect that he's not saying all that's on his mind and worry if he's "hiding something."

Make a pact with each other that you will not let unspoken subtext confuse your conversations. It's better to simply state outright what your inner concerns or conflicts are. For example:

- "If I seem nervous it's because I still tend to read between the lines of what you say. I'm never sure you're speaking everything that's on your mind. Give me time."
- "You've noticed me being quiet. I get that way when I see you get impatient with the kids. You have a right to—kids can be frustrating. But you expected me to patiently learn to trust you after your affair yet you don't seem to work at being more patient."
- "Sometimes I feel guilty about the affair so I don't assert myself when I should and then I get resentful. I have to try to manage my guilt better."
- "I still worry when you don't come home on time but I don't think it's fair anymore for me to question you about it. That's why I seem strained when you come home late."
- "Even though we have many good days now, sometimes I think about how close we came to losing everything because of your affair. So even if we're having fun there are moments I'm somewhat angry. Bear with me."

If such comments are not met with disapproval but are accepted and understood, you can actually feel more close to each other—despite inner conflicts—because you shared those thoughts.

Intimacy Through Touch

After an affair, you and your mate will be very self-conscious in the bedroom. In the roller coaster phase when emotions are high and confusing, nothing that happens (or doesn't happen) sexually will feel right. You already have strong mixed feelings. You might be disgusted by him and not want him to touch you—but you fear losing him if you can't be sexual. Or you might want him to make love to you so you can be reassured of his desire for you—but fear the vulnerability that lovemaking brings. He may do nothing right. If he approaches you for sex you might think, *That's all that's on his mind. He's so insensitive to what I've been through!* If he doesn't approach you for sex (he might be afraid it will annoy you—or perhaps you've rejected his recent advances) you might think, *He's not attracted to me! He's still thinking about HER!*

For his part, if he wants to reconcile with you then making love is—for him, anyway—a safer form of intimacy since it doesn't involve talking. But if the relationship is still highly volatile he may prefer to give you plenty of room and not push for sex—while feeling inadequate to bridge the intimacy gap. If he still has feelings for the other woman, he may miss his physical relationship with her—even if he is clear that he wants to be with you. He may have difficulty becoming aroused with you due to his own fear that if he doesn't do everything "right" you will think he's still cheating on you. (Anxiety will interfere with his sexual performance.) You may regard his difficulty getting an erection when with you as evidence that he is not attracted to you. Many men try to prove to their spouses that they still love them by pursuing them for even more sex. Women may interpret that in a negative light—that all she is to him is a sexual object. And if sex was his primary way of connecting to you before his affair, you will think that nothing substantial has changed and that the relationship is still at risk for some future affair.

And no matter how hard you try to not let it be that way, the other woman will be the third person in bed with you for some time. Both of you will be thinking of her—longingly, fearfully, guiltily, or angrily—which will make any effort at lovemaking less than ideal.

Sex after the Affair

The culprit for you and your mate is always anxiety. Because you are worried and uncertain about where the relationship is headed and what your partner's truest desires are, your actions will be inconsistent and contradictory. You'll pull him closer one day and push him away the next (and he'll respond with similar confusion). How are you *supposed* to think and act? Which thoughts that you have are true and which are distortions? How can you act in ways that help you and yet don't make you vulnerable to being hurt again? The answer to all those questions is this: *You must ACCEPT that your thoughts, feelings, and actions will be confused and contradictory. You must ALLOW contradictory beliefs and desires to peacefully coexist for now. You must not attempt to oversimplify your situation by acting as if one set of beliefs is true and another set is false when fear is fueling your judgment.* So, for example, if your husband wants to make love and you have mixed feelings, instead of making love and then regretting it—or instead of rejecting his advances and then regretting it—allow both sides of what you feel to be true. Making love or not making love is less important than how you deal with that choice. So you might say, for example:

- "I'm not ready for that at the moment. Part of me wants to and I know you're trying to get closer to me. I'll let you know when I'm more ready."

Or, you might say,

- "Okay, but please understand I still have many mixed emotions. I may or may not feel as close to you as you'd like afterward. But I do want us to make the attempt."

That is why Chapter 4 on emotional acceptance is so important. When feelings are mixed it's best to accept all of your feelings rather than try to eliminate some of them through force of logic or willpower.

You want closeness and you don't want it. You love him and you're furious with him. You can't trust him entirely but you know you must give him chances to prove his trust. You want him to know you're still hurt and angry and you want him to continue to believe in your future together. The worst thing you can do is act on both sides of your feelings at different times. He will not be able to predict your actions so will likely pull back and not take the chance of upsetting you or getting rejected—and you will see that as a sign that he doesn't care. The best thing to do is make a choice of how to act at that moment while indicating that your feelings are mixed and that you understand he's trying to make the best of a bad situation.

The same is true for shows of affection as it is for sex. You might want affection but flinch or pull away if he offers it. Say: "I want us to be more affectionate and at the same time I'm hurt and worried. Bear with me if I don't always respond the way you'd hope."

Intimacy Through Togetherness

Occupying the same room and breathing the same air isn't the same thing as togetherness. Togetherness involves doing things together that are fun, pleasurable, or interesting so that the two of you feel close. After an affair, building intimacy through togetherness may be simpler than building intimacy through sex, affection, or conversation. There's less room for error. Conflict per se doesn't create relationship dissatisfaction. The absence of positive emotions is the key element. After an affair positive emotions take a nosedive. Even a conflict-free relationship—if it's accompanied by a lack of positive emotions—is a dead relationship.

Rebuilding positive feelings can take a major step forward if you and your spouse increase the amount of togetherness that is conflict-free and enjoyable. A romantic getaway is probably not a good idea so soon after the disclosure of an affair. Chances are neither of you will be in the best mood to take advantage of the opportunity. Small outings are a good idea. Even something as bland as going grocery shopping together can be fine if it starts out as breakfast in a restaurant first. Go for walks together while holding hands. Look in your local newspaper for things to do in your region over the weekend—things that you wouldn't ordinarily do but that you might enjoy. These outings are not the times to have confrontations or debates. If you talk about the status of your relationship, keep the conversation simple and brief and focus more on what you'd like to get out of the day or in upcoming outings. Save serious discussion for another time and place.

You may have mixed feelings about doing something fun with your partner when you feel so lousy. Again, the goal is to push the envelope and aim for some degree of pleasantness together. Have modest but positive expectations.

These are good moments for each of you to ask, "What's it like for him (or her) having me around right now?" If the answer is more negative than positive, try to shift it in the other direction.

Making progress in any one of the four pathways to intimacy makes it easier to make gains in the other areas. During the rebuilding phase of your post-affair relationship, make an intimacy pact with your mate. It should contain these elements:

- I will continue (or improve) efforts at intimacy every day when possible.
- I won't allow ordinary day-to-day hassles and stresses to interfere with intimacy.
- I will focus more on what I need to do to sustain intimacy, not on what my partner needs to do.
- Setbacks are common but I will get back on track quickly.

Intimacy doesn't just happen—it must be cultivated.

forging a forgiving heart: releasing anger and opening to love

Repeat this phrase to yourself and take special notice of your gut reaction: *It's important to forgive him for what he did.*

Was your gut reaction one of disgust, anger, or dismay? Or did you feel more positive about the idea? If your reaction stirred up feelings of righteous anger, don't worry. That's the most common reaction, especially if the injury against you was recent or very profound. If your reaction to the concept is more negative than positive, chances are one of four possible reasons exists:

1. You have no intention to forgive.
2. You cannot forgive because the affair is still ongoing.
3. You wish to forgive but do not know how.
4. You have the wrong idea of what forgiveness is about.

You can forgive him for his affair but still choose not to have a relationship if you can never trust him again or if he chooses to be with the other woman. But you can't reconcile in your relationship without forgiveness. If you want your relationship to survive and heal, forgiveness needs to happen eventually. While forgiveness is not easy (and when you have been deeply hurt you are entitled to harbor resentment), it may be less difficult than you imagine.

What Is Genuine Forgiveness?

In the immediate aftermath of deep injury and betrayal, offering forgiveness is not usually the first course of action people take, nor should it necessarily be. Forgiveness is a process that typically takes time before any genuine reconciliation can occur. When forgiveness happens quickly after a deep betrayal, it probably wasn't genuine but done out of fear.

According to esteemed researcher Dr. Robert Enright, a pioneer in the scientific study of forgiveness, forgiveness is a process whereby an injured person eventually abandons her right to resentment or retaliation and nurtures more benevolent attitudes such as compassion and generosity—which the perpetrator does not necessarily deserve. A closer look at that definition reveals the following:

- The injury must be acknowledged in full by the injured person, not minimized or distorted. Otherwise, what is really being forgiven?
- Forgiveness must be freely chosen. If one "forgives" out of a pressured sense of obligation it may be a shallow forgiveness.
- Forgiveness is a gift. The perpetrator is not entitled to it.
- Letting go of anger is only part of the forgiveness process. There also needs to be some form of opening of one's heart—even a little—toward the perpetrator with some degree of goodwill, compassion, love, kindness, or generosity. (At a minimum it might be wishing that the perpetrator is able to improve his or her life over time.)

Most people who've been deeply hurt view forgiveness as perpetuating an injustice. Forgiveness somehow let's a perpetrator "get away with it." However, in the case of infidelity, an unfaithful partner who wishes to be reconciled with his partner usually pays a heavy price even if he's eventually forgiven. Months of grief, uncertainty, guilt, despair, and anguish typically occur before he can be forgiven. Gayle Reed, a researcher at the University of Wisconsin, conducted a study of men and women who'd been cheated on. She found that eventually these individuals wanted to let go of their anger and that those who forgave their partners reported significantly less emotional distress and more well-being. So it tends to be true: withholding forgiveness may harm the victim more than the perpetrator over time.

With forgiveness, an offense is never condoned, minimized, or excused. For forgiveness to be genuine, the nature of the hurt must be seen fully for what it is—not sugarcoated.

When It Looks like Forgiveness but It's Not

After two months of anguish and arguments over his affair, Cathy's husband Frank threatened to go back to his girlfriend. He accused Cathy of "pushing me away" by her constant anger. She taunted him to leave. As he was about to, Cathy became frightened she might lose him forever this time. She promised she'd stop the arguing and said the magic words "I forgive you." It wasn't genuine and it didn't help anyway. Within a week her suppressed anger flared and Frank used it as an opportunity to find fault with her inability to "let go of the past" and for being an "unforgiving person."

Forgiveness is not genuine if it stems from fear. Fear will make you deny or minimize the injury. If that happens, and you haven't had time to sort through how it has affected you, you will quickly "forgive" and still suffer from underlying wounds that go untreated. The religious ideal of forgiving one's enemies is valuable. However, if one forgives too quickly so as to avoid offending God, one misses the chance to be truly forgiving.

Some forgive so as to have a weapon to use against the wrongdoer. "I forgave you, so now you owe me." It becomes a way to keep the wrongdoer perpetually in one's debt.

Some believe that forgiveness can only happen if the perpetrator expresses genuine remorse and a desire to be forgiven. Certainly that can make it easier for a victim to offer forgiveness. But forgiveness is a personal response to being injured. It isn't contingent upon another's attitudes. Forgiveness can happen within one's heart without the wrongdoer ever hearing the words—such as when the wrongdoer's whereabouts are unknown. However, it is less likely that there can be a true reconciliation between the individuals if the wrongdoer does not show remorse and apologize. "I forgive you, but I can no longer live with you" may then be a realistic outcome.

If your partner was unfaithful, you may want to consider forgiveness whether or not the two of you are able to reunite. But if reconciliation is the goal, forgiveness needs to occur eventually.

The Phases of Forgiveness

If the affair was very recent, forgiveness may seem a far-off dream and you may be seeking revenge more than forgiveness. If you have passed through the roller coaster stage of recovery and have entered the subdued stage, forgiveness may start to have some kind of appeal. Often, it is only when you have grown weary of the pain of betrayal that the hope forgiveness offers seems palatable.

Forgiveness is more than the expression of words. When you proceed through the forgiveness process you will have dramatically reduced or even eliminated not only negative feelings about the person who betrayed you, but will let go of negative beliefs and negative actions as well. Plus, there will be a corresponding increase in positive feelings, thoughts, and behaviors toward the one who hurt you. Does this mean you must trust him again? No. You can forgive and have reason to mistrust. But if you wish to reconcile the relationship, trust must return.

Is It Wrong to Want Revenge?

Wanting revenge is a normal response to deep, unfair injury. Actively seeking revenge is also common, although it can complicate your life and result in greater misery. It's important to emotionally accept your desire for revenge rather than deny it out of fear of your anger. But revenge must be something you get past if healing is to occur.

My first book, *The Forgiving Marriage* (1989), outlined several phases people typically go through when trying to forgive. Research conducted in the 1990s (and that continues today), primarily by Dr. Bob Enright at the University of Wisconsin (and others, such as psychiatrist Richard Fitzgibbons) added greater clarity to the forgiveness process. Dr. Enright recognized four phases:

1. The uncovering phase
2. The decision phase
3. The work phase
4. The deepening phase

These phases are not automatic and absolute. Some individuals may skip over many of the particulars of a phase and still genuinely forgive. Furthermore, a person often is in more than one phase at a time, although one phase predominates.

The Uncovering Phase

What happened? How did it come about? How have you been hurt? How well can you handle it? Those are the essential questions of this phase. The enormity of what has happened—its full impact on you—usually cannot be determined until some time has passed. The final outcome may be worse or better than you first thought. When you forgive, you forgive a hurt against you. But you need to comprehend exactly what the hurts are. After an affair, the kinds of hurts can be many: loss of safety and security, loss of lovability, loss of esteem, loss of control over your life, loss of a sense of fairness. If you've been betrayed by others in your past (parents, friends, other partners), then the level of your hurt may run deeper. Or you may have numbed yourself emotionally due to past events and be less aware of the impact the hurt against you has now.

In addition to uncovering the impact the affair has had on you, you uncover the facts of the affair. Did he have a sexual affair? An emotional affair? Both? When did it begin? Did he take pleasure in his lies? Did he care at all about you during his affair? Does he exhibit any genuine remorse now? What are his reasons for cheating?

By now you may recognize that many of the events during the roller coaster phase of recovery mirror some of the events in the uncovering phase of forgiveness. It is during this phase that you also begin to take stock of your ability to cope. Are you devastated? Unable to function day to day? Are you able to withstand the pain and function as well as one might despite the fact that your life is in disarray?

Everyone has defense mechanisms that operate during an emotional crisis. Defense mechanisms are best used as temporary measures, not long-term strategies. For example, *displacement* is a defense mechanism whereby anger at someone who caused injury is displaced onto someone else. After an affair, if you are the injured party and were also betrayed in the past by someone else (a parent or lover) you may displace some of that anger on to the partner who recently betrayed you and find it harder to reconcile with him as a result. Or anger that should be directed at the unfaithful spouse is directed instead at others who make you upset or mad (the children, inconsiderate drivers, coworkers, and so on).

Denial is a defense mechanism whereby you deny or minimize the hurt against you. In the short term such a belief may buy you some time, give you a breather, before the hard work of rebuilding your future occurs. But if it goes on too long, you may ignore relationship factors that must be addressed if a true reconciliation can happen.

Or you may set yourself up to be hurt again. Instinctively *blaming yourself* can also be a defense mechanism. Yes, it's possible you contributed to a less-than-happy relationship and you need to evaluate that. But while automatically blaming yourself and excusing him gives you a greater sense of immediate control (it's easier to fix yourself than to fix him if he is to blame), it distorts reality and overlooks his role.

The Decision Phase

When I met Nancy the idea of forgiveness was the last thing on her mind. Her fiancé ended their relationship shortly before their wedding. She had quit a well-paying job in order to relocate to a new state where they were supposed to begin their new life together. Instead, he began his new life with Erin, a woman he'd been secretly involved with for six months.

When I first raised the idea of forgiveness she scoffed. But then she admitted that she was bitter and miserable and nothing else she had tried to do to overcome her pain had worked. *Realizing that nothing else has eliminated your suffering is as good a reason as any to consider forgiveness.*

In order to decide *for* forgiveness, you may need to examine any resistance you have to the idea. What do you think you will lose if you forgive? Many think they lose their personal integrity. They regard forgiveness as a weak thing to do; a caving in of one's self-respect. That may be true if you "forgive" from fear. But refusing to forgive can also be a choice made from fear—fear of being hurt again, fear of losing self-respect, or fear of what others may think.

If you fear that forgiveness will open you up to being hurt again, that isn't true. Reconciling with your partner puts you at risk (but so does any relationship). Failing to forgive requires that you sustain your anger and resentment—which will complicate any other relationship you may enter into. If you wish to be in a loving relationship with anyone, you must be willing to risk being hurt. Otherwise you will hold back your level of devotion so that any hurt will be less painful—but holding back increases the odds the relationship will fail.

If you commit to forgiveness, you must also abandon efforts to seek revenge. You cannot be punitive and vengeful and at the same time be forgiving. This doesn't mean that all of your actions will be loving and kind. You may seek forgiveness and attempt to work on it, but find it hard to completely warm up to the one who betrayed you. That's normal. However, since the process of forgiveness involves opening one's heart to the one who hurt you, your goal is to slowly but surely welcome him back into your life in a more loving way (if there is to be a reconciliation) or to wish him well in your heart (if there is not to be a reconciliation).

The decision phase often takes shape when you are willing to consider forgiveness as an option. But until you commit yourself to the process, it's hard to go on to the next phase with any degree of determination.

The Work Phase

The good news is that you've probably already begun the work phase even though you may not have realized it. Earlier chapters in this book addressed how to change certain unhelpful beliefs and to broaden your coping efforts, all of which will help propel you through this next phase.

The work phase is really about gaining a shift in your perspective. For example, a closeup view of a raging forest fire can seem horrific—until the camera pans back and you see that only a small portion of the forest is affected. Your job now is to view your partner from the perspective of a camera that takes a wide-angle shot. See him in more than just the narrow perspective of someone who was unfaithful and take in all aspects of who he is, his life history, his personality, his strengths and weaknesses, and his fundamental level of goodness.

According to Dr. Enright, there are four major components to the work phase:

1. Understanding the perpetrator.
2. Developing empathy toward him.
3. Feeling compassion for him.
4. Accepting the pain you experienced rather than fighting it.

This process is made more difficult because the manner in which you understand him usually comes from dialogue—and conversations can easily become problematic. (Please re-read Chapter 7 and Chapter 9 in this book for more help in that area.)

Understanding Him Better

Your goal is not to excuse his actions but to more fully *understand them* in the context of your life together, the circumstances affecting him at the time of his betrayal, and his life prior to knowing you. One way of looking at it: *you want to understand him as fully as you would want to be understood by others if you committed a similar act of betrayal.* The language you use to describe him can make all the difference. Is he *unloving* or is he *weak*? Is he *completely untrustworthy* or did he *make a horrible error in judgment*? Is he a *liar* or is he someone *who was afraid to tell the truth*? It's your call. But you must bring to bear *all* that you know about him—his past actions and attitudes—and not judge him solely by his choice to be unfaithful. Black-and-white thinking is another defense mechanism. It eases your anxiety by narrowing your options to two: he's both bad and untrustworthy or he is basically good. But either choice is a distorted and unfair view. Expanding your view of him, making him more three-dimensional, is the harder task—but it's more accurate and fair.

Were circumstances in his life—worries, pressures, losses, and so forth—a possible factor? Again, this is not to excuse him but to discover all of the factors that may have been affecting him. (True, in the final analysis it was his choice to be unfaithful.) The question is that given all you understand about people and life, *do his actions make some kind of sense given the circumstances of his entire life? If he was simply a close friend but not your partner, might you find some kind of sympathy for what he did? Would you still view him as a decent (yet flawed) person?*

It helps in your effort to understand him if he is actively trying to understand himself better. When men who've been unfaithful come to me and sincerely wish to figure out why they did what they did, it's a good sign. Men who don't wish to be introspective and wish instead to get past the affair as quickly as possible offer less reassurance to a mistrusting partner and will likely slow down the reconciliation process.

Developing Empathy for Him

For some people, forgiveness means "I'll stop being angry with you but I could not care less what happens to you from now on." Indifference to the one who hurt you is a limited form of forgiveness (it's for"give"ness without the "give"). Ideally, forgiveness involves both the cessation of resentment *and* the stirrings of some degree (however small) of caring or concern. Developing empathy for the man who betrayed you will help you to feel more forgiving.

Empathy happens when you place yourself in another person's emotional shoes. It's not feeling sorry for him (sympathy) but trying to feel what he feels (and felt)—as much as that is ever possible.

Understanding him better is a foundation for empathy. When you understand him in a larger context than just his affair, you are closer to developing empathy. Empathy sometimes happens when the victim can honestly state "There but for the grace of God go I." In other words, empathy happens when we accept that we ourselves are not above being hurtful or selfish or weak. Had we lived in the shoes of the other, perhaps we'd have made similar poor choices.

You may be thinking, "I'm not perfect but I would *never* betray someone I love like he did." Thus, you may think yourself incapable of having empathy for him in this matter. Please consider the fact that, in my experience, the majority of people who cheated on their partners never believed they would have done so. Also consider that some people may never cheat on a spouse but show character weaknesses in other ways—nasty tones, lack of appreciation, hostile comments, emotional neglect, insensitivity, selfishness, a sense of entitlement to have their way, and so forth. No one is above being unkind or hurtful. It is with that sense of self-understanding that you can perhaps identify in some way with the person who betrayed you and whom you wish to forgive.

Feeling Compassion

Compassion is empathy in action. It is the act of *moving toward* the perpetrator with some degree of kindness or generosity of spirit.

Months after Melissa's husband Dante cheated on her she watched him one night as he got their son ready for bed after giving him a bath. The boy said to his dad, "I like it when you read me stories." Melissa could easily tell what must have been going through Dante's mind. She knew he was worried that she may never be able to forgive him and that his opportunities to read his son bedtime stories might become limited if they were to separate. She saw him swallow hard and knew he was regretting his actions that may cost him his marriage and family life. She decided to make him one of his favorite meals—something she hadn't done in months—as a kind of friendly overture, a way of saying, "I still care about you and I know you are suffering, too." Compassion literally means "suffering *with*." Melissa was able to see that they both suffered as a result of his actions, not just her.

Compassion need not be a gushing forth of positive emotion. Start small. Think of things you can do that might make his day go easier or make him feel a bit more special. Offer small kindnesses when you could easily overlook them. Try to imagine yourself in his position and see if there is any aspect of his situation that you can care about. If so, use that caring as motivation to do something positive for him. Or recall something you are grateful for in this relationship—something from your past together that makes you smile when you think about it—and let that be your motivation to demonstrate some kind of caring or concern.

Accepting the Pain

Ultimately, where forgiveness is concerned, you must "take the hit." That is, you must absorb the pain instead of throwing it back on the offender through acts of vengeance. The cycle of hurting stops with you—even though you're entitled to seek revenge. This is true for anyone wishing to overcome unfairness. Accepting the pain doesn't mean that you must wallow in it or forever feel it. Actually, if you stop fighting the idea that your pain wasn't deserved and that you have a right to be vengeful, you may discover that your pain lessens. Accepting reality, not fighting it, results in relief. Resisting reality keeps pain alive.

Acceptance itself is easy, actually. "I accept that this happened to me even though it wasn't fair." Acceptance is letting go. The work aspect of it involves your inner obstacles to letting go. A strong sense of righteousness ("I can't let him get away with it!") often propels people to remain angry, bitter, or vengeful. Or they're afraid of making themselves vulnerable to being hurt again. Rather than turn those issues into an internal debate ("I should forgive him and accept what happened . . . No! That's not fair!") it's best to accept both sides of the issue ("I accept that I must absorb the pain and I accept that it isn't fair"). By accepting both contrary views, the inner battle is eliminated and acceptance becomes easier.

The Deepening Phase

The meanest form of suffering is suffering with no meaning.

However, you can make your suffering—the pain of betrayal—meaningful. Finding meaning in adversity doesn't mean that the adversity was worth the price. The cost of suffering may seem to outweigh any benefits your suffering may have brought you. Still, when you find meaning in your suffering the pain lessens because the pain is transformed into something new. For example, imagine breaking a leg and being unable to compete in the Olympics. The pain of the broken leg is made worse by the loss of being able to compete in something you worked so hard for. But imagine breaking a leg in the exact same way by saving your child's life. The physical pain would be transformed into something positive and would therefore be more bearable.

Meaningfulness takes root when you consider the *possibility* that because of your suffering you will experience a quality of life you might otherwise have not known. The truth is that adversity can break some people but more often they are stronger for it. As a result of the betrayal will you become a stronger person in the long run? More courageous? More giving? Did it enhance your spiritual life? Will your children learn a valuable life lesson as a result of the way you handled your situation? Did you start a new career or participate in some helping organization as a result of what happened to you?

Often the benefits of a bad situation are not known for many years. You have to wait and see how your life unfolds as a result of what happened to you before you can accurately judge whether it was truly a blessing, a curse, or something in between. If you cultivate an attitude of trust—trust that whatever happens, it can be to your ultimate benefit—then it can be easier to endure hardship. It's only through adversity that the very important qualities many people aspire to— perseverance, courage, faith, hope, love, forgiveness, gratitude, peace of mind—ultimately reveal themselves. Learning forgiveness makes no sense until you've been betrayed; nurturing faith and hope is more meaningful when you have reasons to doubt; developing perseverance happens only when the going gets tough. And love is more deep and profound when you have reason to not love, but choose to do so anyway.

In the deepening phase, you realize more than ever that you too have needed to be forgiven. Some people believe in the law of karma and see forgiving others as important, in part, because some day they too will want to be forgiven.

A Forgiveness Exercise

Sit down and imagine that the person who hurt you is sitting across from you. Repeat the words *I forgive you* and pay close attention to the words that immediately follow. Those words might be *You don't deserve it . . . But I don't know how . . . But I don't want to . . . But I'm still so angry.* Then repeat the words *I forgive you* and once again pay attention to the thought that immediately follows. Repeat this ten to twenty times. You will notice one of two things happening: either your negative feelings will start to diminish, or you will discover that one theme or thought tends to predominate. That theme, if it is negative, is probably your main sticking point. That's the area you want to address so you can somehow move past it. For example, if your theme is the desire for vengeance, you might want to ask yourself: *Is there any foreseeable end to my need for vengeance? What must happen for me to let go of that need?*

Repeat the forgiveness exercise but this time put that one troublesome theme to one side for a moment. Look for other sticking points. Once you find them, ask yourself what could happen to address those concerns so that the forgiveness process can unfold.

The process of forgiveness evolves. Rarely does it happen in a flash. And even if you feel forgiving, it must be demonstrated over time by your actions. Give it time to unfold.

troubleshooter's guide to recovery

Once you learn of a partner's affair, a thousand questions flood your brain. Many of those questions get answered over the course of months but often enough those answers lead to *even more questions*. It can be an exhausting process.

As you proceed with healing, you will notice that you somehow struck a balance between seeking answers to some questions and allowing other questions to remain forever unanswered. For example, there is no answer to the question *"How can I be sure this will never happen again?"* since life rarely offers us certainty about anything. The famous "Serenity Prayer" is very appropriate when coping with the pain of infidelity. Your job is to make changes where you can (in your relationship and yourself), accept that there are some things that cannot be changed, and, hopefully, know which is which.

That being said, the following questions and answers might help you if you get stuck in the process of healing, reconciliation, or moving on from the relationship.

When he tells me his reasons for having an affair it still seems to me he's making excuses. And I feel I'm setting myself up to once again be made a fool of if I believe his excuses in an effort to "understand" him. What should I do?

This is a sticking point for many people. Many betrayed spouses think, "If you truly loved me or cared about me (or the kids) you would never have cheated. Since you did cheat, you must not care." It certainly might be that he no longer cares and he wants out. However, many people who describe themselves as happily married will cheat. And many of them will sincerely want their marriage to survive. His affair was ultimately a choice he made that he must accept responsibility for. But there were factors that led up to that choice. Understanding those factors doesn't make him less guilty. It may help you to see him as more human or perhaps as weak, rather than as cold and unfeeling.

Many people feel humiliated by their partner's affair. They hate being made to look foolish. However, if you wish to reconcile you must take the risk.

We're trying to work things out, but I think he's still lying to me.

Fear and mistrust will automatically make you doubt his words. After all, he lied before about his affair (or withheld the truth by being secretive). A man who still has something to hide (he's still cheating or still in contact with the other woman) will get defensive more quickly in response to your questions. A man who is trying to tell the truth may be frustrated by your doubting him but will understand. A guilty man (or one who hasn't told you the whole story) will turn things around and make you the problem. A man trying to heal the wounds of betrayal will do whatever it takes to convince you. He will go out of his way for you. If he does not, it raises the question that he still might be cheating. If he isn't cheating, it may be that he has an arrogant, controlling personality—which is a problem in itself. (Humility goes a long way toward reconciliation and healing.)

Although I explain to all unfaithful men who wish to repair their marriage to completely come clean, my experience has been that sometimes they will leave out details that they worry will be more hurtful to their partners or will create more turmoil. For example, maybe he told you his affair started two months ago when actually it began seven months ago. He may tell you there was no sexual intercourse when there was. He may stick to those lies believing it will only stir things up to tell the truth now. But then after a month or two of your trying to cope with the affair the truth comes out and it feels like a punch. Now you feel as if you've lost ground. What else has he been lying about? This is where sound judgment comes in on your part. Yes, his continuing to lie was very wrong. But was it done out of fear that you'd be hurt or the reconciliation process would get stalled? Or was he lying because he sees this process as a game and he's trying to get away with something? In other words, what is his essential character? Is he basically a good, decent guy who made a terrible choice and lied to cover it up so things wouldn't get out of hand? Or is he someone whose own ego gets in the way of him being truly remorseful and devoted?

Generally speaking, your man may not be suited for a healthy, mature relationship if in the course of trying to come to terms with his affair he displays several of the following:

- He minimizes what he did.
- He is quick to blame you.
- He views you as controlling or unforgiving when you want answers.
- He accuses you of overreacting.
- He rolls his eyes in contempt when you have questions.
- He responds with a bullying tone.
- He threatens "You'll be sorry!" should you consider leaving him.
- He refuses to allow you complete access to his cell phone, e-mails, etc.

In the aftermath of an affair the betrayed partner wants the whole truth. The problem is that you can never know when you have the entire story. But you can have enough of the story for you to make a determination as to whether or not you can continue in the relationship.

Three months after I discovered his affair I learned of a detail he'd never mentioned. When I confronted him he said, "I forgot." How does he expect me to ever believe anything he tells me?

The primary source of pain after an affair is not just the sexual betrayal. The deeper hurt is lack of trust and the deceit that created it. So when a man says "I forgot," it stirs up fears of more deceit. If his efforts to heal the relationship until now have been sincere and not halfhearted I would give him the benefit of the doubt. Anxiety interferes with memory (ever freeze up when taking a test or giving a public speech?). It's very likely that he did forget. Be careful of the pattern where he reveals new information and you accuse him of having been deceitful for not having revealed it earlier. He may then think twice about telling you details he remembers later on, fearing you will hold it against him.

Are there any questions I shouldn't ask him?

Detailed questions about his lover may cause you more harm than good. Asking what she looked like, what she does for a living, was she married, and other "facts" may be okay. I caution you against asking questions that may make you feel worse. *Was she better in bed than me? What kinds of things did you do together in bed? Did you find her more attractive than me?* If he downplays her appeal, you won't believe him. If he answers that she was terrific in all ways you'll feel lousy. Don't ask rhetorical questions that have no real answer. There is no answer he can provide to the question *How could you do this to me?* that will make you respond, "Oh, I understand completely." Other questions to avoid: *Did you think of her today? Do you ever think fondly of her? Do you ever wonder what life would be like with her instead of me?* Chances are all those answers are in the affirmative. Don't be a masochist.

We're getting a divorce. Should the children know it's because he had an affair?

If he has every intention of staying with the other woman and she will become a part of the children's lives, yes they need to know about her. Any discussion of the other woman should be done without hostility in front of the kids. "Mommy and daddy aren't happy with each other anymore and daddy wants to be with someone else" is a straightforward way to begin. If the affair ended your marriage but he has no interest in being with the other woman, there may be no need to mention her.

Should we stay together for the sake of the kids?

According to the cumulative evidence in many research studies, children are better off if the parents remain together *as long as* there is little fighting in the household. If the parents argue a lot or if there is some other dysfunction as a result of the marital unhappiness (chronic depression, alcoholism, and so forth) children are probably damaged by the parents remaining together as much as they will be harmed by the divorce.

If you are unsure if you want your marriage to survive after an infidelity, working on salvaging the marriage for the children's sake is a good motive. Many people also try to work things out—when they'd rather call it quits—because they can't afford to separate or they don't wish to change their lifestyle or social network. Those are not ideal reasons to *remain* in a troubled marriage but they may be worthwhile reasons to try to save a troubled marriage in the hope that it will flourish later on.

Can his affair make our marriage better?

Not quite. Yes, your marriage may indeed take on new life after his affair and the two of you may end up with a marriage that's stronger than it was before. But the affair didn't make that happen. The affair caused an upheaval that forced the two of you to bring to bear all you had at your disposal to see if your marriage could not only survive but thrive. You deserve credit for the hard work you put into making the marriage better. Don't give the affair credit.

How do I stop obsessing about what he did? I can't stop my brain!

It can be helpful to spend about thirty minutes a day for at least four consecutive days writing out your obsessive thoughts. Research findings indicate that the very act of writing out one's thoughts and feelings results in a lessening of obsessive preoccupation.

Imagine that the affair and the sex was part of an actual movie playing at your local theater. Would it truly excite the masses? Without makeup and perfectly proportioned young bodies, was your guy's romp in the hay with that other woman really an eye-popping experience? Since it's all your imagination, you can change the image. Imagine it as a photograph, perhaps snapped at just the moment when they were at their most awkward or least flattering positions. If you prefer a more spiritual focus, imagine the image being bleached out by an ever-expanding white, angelic light. With enough repetition, you change the upsetting image to a more neutral one—or even an absurd one.

I've forgiven him but how do I get my parents to forgive him?

You may not be able to. They may be harboring their own personal hurts from the past—for example, maybe your mother felt betrayed by a member of her family while growing up—and your husband's affair triggered reminders in them. Still, it can help if he apologizes to them as well. He did not hurt them the way you were hurt, but they probably suffered as they worried about you and your future and perhaps your children's future. They may feel let down by him, especially if they always treated him warmly and were generous toward him.

Ask them to take the high road and treat him politely as long as you have made the choice to stay with him.

We will still run into the other woman from time to time. How should I handle that?

Your best bet is to ignore her whenever possible. You and your husband should have an agreement that on occasions when all three of you are in the same place together, he will stand by your side and make it clear that he is with you by his actions. If an encounter with her cannot be avoided (due to job or social obligations), keep any conversation extremely brief, civil, and move on as quickly as possible. Your husband should not engage in "friendly" conversation with this woman.

The other woman has called me and told me things my husband denies. Who do I believe?

You have to determine who has more of a motive to tell the truth or to lie. Does she want him back? She may tell you untruths so your relationship will suffer—although she risks his wrath in doing so. If she is angry at him for leaving her, she may tell you untruths so as to make him pay a price. You must examine your husband's recent efforts. Does it seem as if he's been trying to reconcile with you and be as honest as possible? Or has he been preoccupied, less enthusiastic, and not very informative when you ask him questions? The truth will reveal itself in time if you are willing to wait. If he truly wishes to be with her, he probably will. If not, his efforts to prove to you his devotion will remain fairly strong.

There are no guarantees, but what things can we do to improve the odds there won't be another affair?

The main thing is open communication. You should be able to talk regularly and openly about your lives and how your relationship

225

is doing. It's important to have "progress checks" after a marital crisis. If conversations become less frequent and you sense he is preoccupied with things but not confiding in you, that bad habit needs to be broken.

You might try getting into some routine you both enjoy. For example, you might go out for a stroll several nights a week and chat. Or make sure that you enjoy breakfast together every Sunday morning (or more often, if possible). Or you may schedule a regular date night. Regular time together ensures you have time to talk and stay connected.

When we discuss his affair I can't help getting very hostile. How can I better manage my emotions at those times? He tells me that unless I calm down he'll refuse to talk.

In the long run, the more hostile you remain, the less likely any dialogues you have will be satisfying and lead to healing. I suggest that for now you limit conversations to about thirty minutes at a time. During those thirty minutes, divide the time up into three five-minute segments each. During your first five minutes you are allowed to speak uninterrupted. Your best bet is not to come at him like a hail of gunfire, but limit what you say to one or two key things you want him to understand. Then he has five minutes to respond—uninterrupted. In your next five minutes you can respond to what he just said or bring up new points—whatever you wish. Then he has five minutes, and so on. This method can make any outbursts more bearable since interruptions won't inflame the situation.

I find it difficult to make love with him now. I imagine him doing it with HER and that taints my experience. Or I feel that by allowing us to make love I'm giving him the impression that everything is okay with us when it isn't. But if I don't make love, I'm afraid he'll wish he was with her. How do I feel better?

You need to view making love not as a sign that all is well, but simply as the fulfillment of your wish now, at this moment, to make love. No more, no less. It is what it is—don't make it into something it isn't. You can certainly let him know that when you make love it is still awkward and difficult for you and that you may not want to on some occasions. But tell him you make love as part of your effort to try to rebuild the relationship, not as an indication that everything's just fine.

Bad memories can be replaced by better ones. As you and your husband get back on track and the relationship improves, thoughts of her will become less intrusive.

He told me he put me out of his mind when he was with the other woman; that he tried not to think about me. What should I make of that?

He's describing a defense mechanism known as *compartmentalization*. When he did that, he knew he was cheating on you and what he was doing was wrong, but he put his thoughts of you inside a different compartment in his brain. Men tend to be better at this than women. "Out of sight, out of mind" is a phrase that describes compartmentalization. It isn't a sign of his character but more an indication of how he deals with things he'd rather not face. During the repair phase of an affair, your man might want to pay attention to how often he compartmentalizes (he watches the game on TV and doesn't think to ask you if you need help with the kids when you've obviously got your hands full) and try to put himself in your shoes more often.

He's agreed to work on the marriage but I know his heart is with her. He's miserable at home. Should I let him go?

If he had feelings for her he will absolutely miss her if he ends their relationship. His misery is probably a combination of sadness at the loss, sadness at the mess he's made, guilt, anxiety about the future, and perhaps anger at himself, you, or the situation. Combine that with the fact that all of your mutual efforts to repair things are happening with a cloud over your heads. You're not a happy couple at the moment. If he maintains his distance from her it may take weeks or months before she is—for the most part—out of his system. Your best bet then is to let him know you understand even though it isn't easy to have sympathy for him.

If he's pining away for her because he'd truly rather be with her, your choice is to let him go or wait until he makes that choice. There is no formula for that decision. You have to decide what you can handle—waiting for the inevitable (but hoping for the best) or taking action.

I think I understand about emotional acceptance, but I find it hard to do. I DON'T accept what he did. Any suggestions?

You might be misunderstanding the concept. To emotionally accept something doesn't mean it's morally acceptable. It means that you stop arguing against the reality of what happened. Some people think that if they still feel bad they must not be accepting the situation. You can accept that something happened and still have sadness about it. It's okay to say, "I don't like what happened but I accept that it happened." If you're still struggling with the concept, tell yourself, "I accept that I can't accept it right now." That is better than continuing to wrestle with the concept.

What should we expect from therapy if we seek counseling together?

The therapist may spend a session or two gathering preliminary information about your current crisis, the overall history of your marriage, and background information. Then the therapist should give you some guidelines as to what the next sessions will accomplish. He or she may wish to meet with the two of you individually for a session as well. The first thing that needs to be assessed is your levels of commitment to working on the marriage and recovering from the affair. One or both of you may not be highly committed, which will definitely impede progress. Still, it can be useful to allow the therapy session to be a forum in which difficult issues and opinions can be discussed. Better to know where you stand as a couple than be in the dark.

If the goal is to reconcile, therapy will be a juggling act between coping with the immediate aftermath of the affair and trying to broaden the focus to other pertinent areas such as communication skills, the state of the relationship prior to the affair, and so forth.

You may or may not meet weekly. As you progress you may meet less often to give you time in between sessions to make progress on your own.

What if he won't attend counseling?

I suggest you give yourselves a time frame within which you will try to make headway on your relationship. If that time passes and there has been little progress, trying couple's counseling is a good idea. Certainly, if your efforts to make improvements are having the opposite effect and things are getting worse, it's better to set up an appointment as soon as possible.

I don't care what you say. Forgiving him feels like I'm caving in and taking it. Doesn't NOT forgiving him make sense?

Not forgiving him makes perfect sense. And the process of forgiveness—especially when it involves a very deep hurt—usually takes time precisely because the injured party needs time to sort through her feelings about what happened and why. My first comment to people who've been betrayed is not "Forgive" but "Tell me more." I want to understand, not offer advice that can't be acted upon.

If you wish to reconcile in your relationship then you'll need to open your heart to at least the *possibility* of forgiveness. If you wish to end the relationship and move on, you're under no obligation to forgive him. But you will be left with resentment and mistrust and those emotions may indeed affect you in your next relationship. So forgiveness is really for your sake, not his.

As stated earlier in the book, forgiveness needn't be this warm, fuzzy glow of love. It may simply begin as a willingness to wish him well in his life and to release your anger—which you're entitled to hold on to—so as to make your burden lighter.

While we might be able to work things out, his affair has permanently changed my view of our relationship. It feels like it will be forever scarred, like a crack in a mirror. Should I think that way or am I being too sensitive?

Yes, some people regard their marriage after an affair as "damaged goods." His affair ruined your dream of having a faithful partner.

Whenever a particular thought distresses me, I've learned to question that thought. Whenever I tell myself that something "should" be a certain way, I wonder if that is really true. We think we know what's in our best interests but do we? It's easy to say that an affair is painful and wrong and should never have happened. But can one truly know that it was not for their betterment somehow?

I prefer to take a spiritual focus on matters when things "go wrong." If you believe you possess a soul, as I do, could it be that something that is wrong in your life might be of some benefit to your soul? Does your soul need to learn something? Experience something? Overcome something? If you ask yourself "How can I become a better person given what has happened to me?" then perhaps your soul will benefit even if your ego takes a hit. Is that a good tradeoff?

But how do you know that your soul benefits when something goes wrong? Maybe you're just deluding yourself.

I'd rather feel better than worse, more positive than pessimistic. If your partner had an affair—and you've had time to process it—ask yourself this question: *If I truly believed that my soul would benefit from this awful experience, how would I feel?* Chances are you'd feel *better.* You'd say that maybe it was worth the pain. Can you absolutely know that that's true? No. But can you be sure it isn't? No. History is filled with stories of people who suffered and somehow rose above it and became better for it. They turned their pain into something beneficial. Think about how you can be a better person as a result of his affair. By making something positive come out of something negative, you're helping yourself cope in a very healthy, mature way.

index

F

Faithfulness, 175
Family
  telling your, about affair, 35–36
  tension between spouse and your,
    139–41, 224
Fear, 4, 34, 202
Financial issues, 172
Forgiveness
  decision phase of, 207–8
  deepening phase of, 213–14
  defining, 200–203
  difficulty of, 31
  exercise, 215
  by family members, 224
  lack of, 230–31
  need for, 200
  phases of, 203–15
  uncovering phase of, 205–6
  work phase of, 208–13
Friends
  affairs by, 83
  telling your, about affair, 36
Future
  assumptions about, 8–9
  belief in, 162–64

G

Goodwill, 185, 188
Gratitude, 161–62
Grief, 4–5, 50, 172–73
Guilt, 4, 7, 192–94

H

Happiness, levels of, 151–53
Healing beliefs, 157–64
Helplessness, 4
Hope, 163–64
Hostility, 226
Humiliation, 4
Husband
  acceptance of responsibility by, 43,
    167–70
  apologies by, 146–47
  assumptions about, 7–8
  attitude of unfaithful, 12
  belief in love of, 66
  civility toward, 82–84
  communicating with, 96–112
  ending of affair by, 42–43
  evasiveness by, 68–69
  feelings of, toward mistress, 120–22,
    228
  feelings of shame by, 69–70
  indecision by, 98–100
  lying by, 66–67, 174–75, 219–21
  personal flaws in, 24–26
  reasons for cheating by, 22–31,
    109–10, 218–19
  remorse by, 43–44, 67–68
  restrictions on, 44, 78–81, 168–72
  trustworthiness of, 173–75
  understanding actions of, 209–10
  understanding character of, 72–73
  unrealistic demands on, 37–38

about the author

Dr. Paul Coleman is a psychologist in private practice. In his twenty-plus years of experience, he has conducted more than 40,000 therapy sessions. He is the author of twelve books including *We Need to Talk: Tough Conversations with Your Spouse* and *The 30 Secrets of Happily Married Couples.*

Dr. Coleman is a member of the American Psychological Association, The Association for Marriage and Family Therapy, the Anxiety Disorders Association of America, and EMDRIA (the international association of EMDR therapists).

He is a public speaker and has appeared on national television shows such as *Oprah* and *The Today Show,* as well as dozens of radio programs across the country.

He and his wife recently celebrated their twenty-fifth wedding anniversary and they have three children.

Visit his website at Paul-Coleman.com.

other books by the author

"We Need to Talk": Tough Conversations with Your Spouse. From Money to Infidelity, Tackle Any Topic with Sensitivity and Smarts. Adams Media, 2008.

The 30 Secrets of Happily Married Couples, Completely revised and updated. Adams Media, 2006.

The Complete Idiot's Guide to Intimacy. Alpha Books, 2005.

How to Say It™ For Couples: Communicating with Tenderness, Openness, and Honesty. Prentice Hall, 2002.

How to Say It™ To Your Child When Bad Things Happen: Good Answers to Tough Questions. Prentice Hall, 2002.

How to Say It™ To Your Kids: The Right Words to Solve Problems, Soothe Feelings, and Teach Values. Prentice Hall, 2000.

Where the Balloons Go. Illustrated by Elizabeth Wilda. Centering Corporation, 1995.